POEMS TO READ

POEMS
TO READ

A NEW FAVORITE POEM

PROJECT ANTHOLOGY

EDITED BY

ROBERT PINSKY
AND MAGGIE DIETZ

W. W. NORTON & COMPANY

NEW YORK   LONDON

For information about permission to reproduce selections from this book, write
to Permissions, W. W. Norton & Company, Inc., 500 Fifth Avenue,
New York, NY 10110

The text and display of this book are composed in Adobe Garamond
Composition by Carole Desnoes
Manufacturing by Maple-Vail Book Manufacturing Group
Book design by Mary A. Wirth
Production manager: Julia Druskin

Library of Congress Cataloging-in-Publication Data

Poems to read : a new favorite poem project anthology / edited by Robert
Pinsky and Maggie Dietz.— 1st ed.
p. cm.
Includes index.
ISBN 0-393-01074-0
1. Poetry—Translations into English. 2. English poetry. 3. American
poetry. I. Pinsky, Robert. II. Dietz, Maggie.
PN6101 .P497 2002
808.81—dc21
2002000321

W. W. Norton & Company, Inc., 500 Fifth Avenue, New York, N.Y. 10110
www.wwnorton.com

W. W. Norton & Company Ltd., Castle House, 75/76 Wells Street, London
W1T 3QT

1 2 3 4 5 6 7 8 9 0

CONTENTS

CHAPTER 4

IN DURANCE SOUNDLY CAGED

CHAPTER 5

CURLED AROUND THESE IMAGES

CHAPTER 6
ALIVE WITH MANY SEPARATE MEANINGS

CHAPTER 7

I MADE MY SONG A COAT

ACKNOWLEDGMENTS

Many organizations and individuals have contributed to the success of the Favorite Poem Project since it began in 1997. This book exists thanks to their efforts.

The editors are grateful first to the eighteen thousand people who have sent us letters or e-mails about their favorite poems, to those who were part of the anthology *Americans' Favorite Poems* (W. W. Norton, 2000) and to the fifty people who appear in the Favorite Poem video documentaries. The videos, and hundreds of Favorite Poem readings around the country, have inspired and guided our work as editors.

The National Endowment for the Arts provided major support for the creation of the videos, which were made under the direction of our invaluable executive producer, Juanita Anderson of Legacy Productions. Thanks are also due to the White House Millennium Council and to the John S. and James L. Knight Foundation, the William and Flora Hewlett Foundation, and to the Charles H. Revson Foundation for their support. We thank *The NewsHour with Jim Lehrer*, which by broadcasting the Favorite Poem videos has made them available to a national audience.

We extend deep thanks to our organizational partners: Boston University, our administrative home, where support and encouragement from Jon Westling and John Silber have made the project possible, and where Lee Indrisano and Stephan Ellenwood, of the School of Education, have helped us reach teachers and students; the Library of Congress and the Center for the Book, which continue to support the project's efforts; the New England Foundation for the Arts, which got us started; and KIDSNET, our new partner for education, whose executive director Karen Jaffe has provided valuable guidance. We are grateful for funding from the Carnegie Corporation, the Massachusetts Foundation for the Humanities and the Tiny Tiger Foundation in support of the project's education and outreach efforts.

Finally, we thank Christine Bauch and Rosemarie Ellis for their years of collegial dedication and wisdom; and Emily Brandt, Jake Cumsky-Whitlock, James Jayo, Caryn O'Connell, and Jill McDonough who contributed valuable efforts to this book.

M.D., R.P.

INTRODUCTION

The young poet John Keats, on February 19, 1818, begins a letter to his friend Reynolds with some thoughts about reading:

> My Dear Reynolds,
> I have an idea that a man might pass a very pleasant life in this manner—let him on any certain day read a certain Page of full Poesy or distilled Prose and let him wander with it, and muse upon it, and reflect from it, and bring home to it, and prophesy upon it, and dream upon it—until it becomes stale—but when will it do so? Never—When Man has arrived at a certain ripeness in intellect any one grand and spiritual passage serves him as a starting post towards all the "two-and-thirty Pallaces."

These sentences, characteristically playful and profound, call up the meaning of this book's title, and the spirit we editors have tried to make our guide.

A poem to *read*, in Keats's sense of the word here, offers a particular pleasure: an act that is as free as wandering, yet purposeful as bringing something home; as intuitive as musing, yet conscious as reflection; as authoritative as prophecy, yet unwilled as dreaming—all possibly happening at once, in such a rush of verbs and prepositions that Keats's sentence, like the process of reading the sentence imitates, seems for a moment to collapse in fatigue. But "in the ripeness of intellect" reading the poem is after all inexhaustible, and finally you start out from it, toward all the palaces of the imagination.

The first anthology to come from the Favorite Poem Project, *Americans' Favorite Poems,* is now in its eighth printing. That book presents a variety of poems, each accompanied by quotations from readers who found in a particular poem something to muse or reflect upon, or bring home to, or prophecy upon, or go beyond staleness in other ways. As with the video segments produced by the project, a process of editorial selection and judgment, choosing among many thousands of letters, underlay *Americans' Favorite Poems.*

That book's purpose was, in the words of its introduction, "to represent the variety and interest of the letters received by the Favorite Poem Project while also making an anthology of literary interest." Part of the first anthology's method was "that the two kinds of interest illuminate one another: that the diversity of readers may give some insight into the poems, and that the sometimes surprising selections of particular poems, breaking stereotypes, may enrich the perception of Americans."

This time, the editors take a more active role in the conversation. Like the first anthology, *Poems to Read* includes poems selected by FPP participants, along with what they say about the poem. For this book, we have selected a number of poems ourselves, often adding our own brief comments. We have also arranged the poems into sections thematically. The selections and comments of the participants are central, and our contributions have been guided by them, in trying to make this volume an effective avenue into the "delicious diligent Indolence" that Keats, a bit later in his February 19 letter to Reynolds, associates with the pleasure of poetry.

In the diverse, rapidly shifting culture of the United States, arts like poetry are not cared for and handed on by a single, unifying folk culture. Nor is poetry curated by an aristocracy or a high bourgeoisie for whom art might have snob value. In place of the folk culture or the aristocratic curatorship, we eagerly improvise institutions: creative writing courses are one example; the Favorite Poem Project is another. The nature of this second anthology extends the process, with the editors overtly and explicitly offering our knowledge and our choices of poems "to read"—in the sense of "recommended" as well as "readable."

In keeping with all of those senses of "poems to read," we found it important to present many poems with no headnote or commentary at all—neither the personal statements by participants nor our own incidental remarks. By no means did we want to imply that instructional headnotes are essential, as they might be in a different book. Our choices of when to add a few words of commentary have been casual, personal, and arbitrary.

Perhaps more than in some societies, we depend upon American schools to keep arts alive and available. Even jazz and film are taught, studied, and protected in schools. Without meaning to produce a textbook, we have tried to make a book that will offer the reader ways to learn more about the satisfactions of poetry and the life in specific poems. If this book is used in schools, we will be pleased; if it were used only in schools, we would be disappointed.

Like the Favorite Poem Project itself, our selection and arrangement of poems and our comments emphasize a specific, vital area: the relation between a poem and a reader, as we "wander with it, and muse upon it, and reflect from it, and bring home to it, and prophesy upon it, and dream upon it—until it becomes stale—but when will it do so? Never."

R.P.
Truro, Massachusetts
July 2001

CHAPTER 1

THERE WAS A CHILD
WENT FORTH

YEHUDA AMICHAI

ISRAEL • 1924–2000

It is such a touching tribute—I wish I could have honored my father in this way. My father did not have an easy life. He never had to fight a war, but he did have his own personal battles to fight. Throughout his life, no matter what, my father maintained his dignity. He taught me to care for my fellow human beings, who are created in the image of God.

—Judy Meltzer, 61, Director of Adult Jewish Learning Center, Baltimore, Maryland

My Father

The memory of my father is wrapped up in
white paper, like sandwiches taken for a day at work.

Just as a magician takes towers and rabbits
out of his hat, he drew love from his small body,

and the rivers of his hands
overflowed with good deeds.

Translated from the Hebrew by Azila Talit Reisenberger

ELIZABETH BISHOP

UNITED STATES • 1911–1979

I love this poem for lots of reasons having to do with technical brilliance and expressive language, but mostly because it's about a child and a grandmother, and how that relationship can contain three worlds: the world of the grandmother, which she relates to the child; the world of the child, which the grandmother sees through the child's enthusiasms; and the vast, shared, private world of the two. I loved my grandmother as much as I've loved anyone. She was born and raised in the southwest corner of Georgia and rarely left that corner of the world. She was independent, self-reliant, generous, and wise; she had more capacity for solitude than anyone I've ever known. I was lucky enough to spend nearly every Saturday of my college years with her, at her small house in Thomasville. I ate her fried chicken and fried okra and black-eyed peas and cornbread and pound cake and divinity fudge, and heard stories about the Depression, about my parents, about the grandfather who'd died thirty years before. She never cried as the grandmother in the poem cries, at least not in front of me. After she died I think I did a fair share of her crying for her. And when I read this poem, I get back some of our time together.

—Mark Mobley, 34, Music Producer, Washington, D.C.

Sestina

September rain falls on the house.
In the failing light, the old grandmother
sits in the kitchen with the child
beside the Little Marvel Stove,
reading the jokes from the almanac,
laughing and talking to hide her tears.

She thinks that her equinoctial tears
and the rain that beats on the roof of the house
were both foretold by the almanac,
but only known to a grandmother.

The iron kettle sings on the stove.
She cuts some bread and says to the child,

It's time for tea now; but the child
is watching the teakettle's small hard tears
dance like mad on the hot black stove,
the way the rain must dance on the house.
Tidying up, the old grandmother
hangs up the clever almanac

on its string. Birdlike, the almanac
hovers half open above the child,
hovers above the old grandmother
and her teacup full of dark brown tears.
She shivers and says she thinks the house
feels chilly, and puts more wood in the stove.

It was to be, says the Marvel Stove.
I know what I know, says the almanac.
With crayons the child draws a rigid house
and a winding pathway. Then the child
puts in a man with buttons like tears
and shows it proudly to the grandmother.

But secretly, while the grandmother
busies herself about the stove,
the little moons fall down like tears
from between the pages of the almanac
into the flower bed the child
has carefully placed in the front of the house.

Time to plant tears, says the almanac.
The grandmother sings to the marvellous stove
and the child draws another inscrutable house.

EAVAN BOLAND

IRELAND • B. 1944

The poet, whose father was a diplomat, was born in Ireland but spent six years of her early childhood in England—to her "a strange country" that in the 1950s was not always welcoming to the Irish. The child listens from her bedroom to the adults playing a card game in the other room. The line framed by "quarreling" and "clattering" clicks like cards being laid down. The child's game is imaginary—a dream of flight. At school, the King she prays for is real, though foreign, the archangels frozen in stone.

—M.D.

The Game

Outside my window an English spring was
summoning home its birds and a week-long fog
was tattering into wisps and rags and at last
I could see the railings when I looked out.

I was a child in a north-facing bedroom in
a strange country. I lay awake listening to
quarreling and taffeta creaking and the clattering
of queens and aces on the inlaid card table.

I played a game: I hid my face in the pillow
and put my arms around it until they thickened.
Then I was following the thaw northward and the air
was blond with frost and sunshine and below me

was only water and the shadow of flight in it
and the shape of wings under it, and in the hours
before morning I would be drawn down and drawn
down and there would be no ground under me

and no safe landing in the dawn breaking on
a room with sharp corners and surfaces on which

the red-jacketed and cruel-eyed fractions of chance
lay scattered where the players had abandoned them.

Later on I would get up and go to school in
the scalded light which fog leaves behind it;
and pray for the King in chapel and feel dumbly for
the archangels trapped in their granite hosannas.

JORGE LUÍS BORGES

ARGENTINA • 1899–1986

Dreamtigers

When I was a child, I came to worship tigers with a passion: not the yellow tigers of the Paraná River and the tangle of the Amazon but the striped tiger, the royal tiger of Asia, which can only be hunted by armed men from a fort on the back of an elephant. I would hang about endlessly in front of one of the cages in the Zoo; and I would prize the huge encyclopedias and books of natural history for the magnificence of their tigers. (I can still recall these illustrations vividly—I, who have trouble recalling the face or the smile of a woman.) My childhood passed and my passion for tigers faded, but they still appear in my dreams. In the unconscious or chaotic dimension, their presences persist, in the following way: While I am asleep, some dream or other disturbs me, and all at once I realize I am dreaming. At these moments, I tend to think to myself: This is a dream, simply an exercise of my will; and since my powers are limitless, I am going to dream up a tiger.

Utter incompetence! My dreaming is never able to conjure up the desired creature. A tiger appears, sure enough, but an enfeebled tiger, a stuffed tiger, imperfect of form, or the wrong size, or only fleetingly present, or looking something like a dog or a bird.

Translated from the Spanish by Alastair Reid

ANNE BRADSTREET

UNITED STATES • 1612–1672

American history is replete with references to our founding fathers. Through those same centuries, America also had founding mothers. Anne Bradstreet is the lynchpin; in her poems, she shares her harsh, yet rich, life. I have two children and, in the future, for them to understand their mother, they must read this poem written by a woman 350 years ago.

—Karen Kline, 52, Writer, North Andover, Massachusetts

To My Dear Children

This book by any yet unread,
I leave for you when I am dead,
That being gone, here you may find
What was your living mother's mind.
Make use of what I leave in love,
And God shall bless you from above.

GWENDOLYN BROOKS

UNITED STATES • 1917–2000

The phrase, "If not an overture, a desecration" is profound, as the conception of "creating" is unsentimental.

—R.P.

Boy Breaking Glass

To Marc Crawford from whom the commission

Whose broken window is a cry of art
(success, that winks aware
as elegance, as a treasonable faith)
is raw: is sonic: is old-eyed première.
Our beautiful flaw and terrible ornament.
Our barbarous and metal little man.

"I shall create! If not a note, a hole.
If not an overture, a desecration."

Full of pepper and light
and Salt and night and cargoes.

"Don't go down the plank
if you see there's no extension.
Each to his grief, each to
his loneliness and fidgety revenge.

Nobody knew where I was and now I am no longer there."

The only sanity is a cup of tea.
The music is in minors.

Each one other
is having different weather.

"It was you, it was you who threw away my name!
And this is everything I have for me."

Who has not Congress, lobster, love, luau,
the Regency Room, the Statue of Liberty,
runs. A sloppy amalgamation.
A mistake.
A cliff.
A hymn, a snare, and an exceeding sun.

SAMUEL TAYLOR COLERIDGE

ENGLAND • 1772–1834

It says what I, as a parent, have always wished for my children: an appreciation of nature, and a spirituality that would allow them to escape from the harshness of life (as complex today, if not more so, than when the poem was written).

—Lucille Ruga, 55, Church Office Ministerial Assistant, St. Petersburg, Florida

Frost at Midnight

    The Frost performs its secret ministry,
Unhelped by any wind. The owlet's cry
Came loud—and hark, again! loud as before.
The inmates of my cottage, all at rest,
Have left me to that solitude, which suits
Abstruser musings: save that at my side
My cradled infant slumbers peacefully.
'Tis calm indeed so calm, that it disturbs
And vexes meditation with its strange
And extreme silentness. Sea, hill, and wood,
This populous village! Sea, and hill, and wood,
With all the numberless goings-on of life,
Inaudible as dreams! the thin blue flame
Lies on my low-burnt fire, and quivers not;
Only that film, which fluttered on the grate,
Still flutters there, the sole unquiet thing.
Methinks its motion in this hush of nature
Gives it dim sympathies with me who live,
Making it a companionable form,
Whose puny flaps and freaks the idling Spirit
By its own moods interprets, everywhere
Echo or mirror seeking of itself,
And makes a toy of Thought.

But O! how oft,
How oft, at school, with most believing mind,
Presageful, have I gazed upon the bars,
To watch that fluttering *stranger!* and as oft
With unclosed lids, already had I dreamt
Of my sweet birthplace, and the old church tower,
Whose bells, the poor man's only music, rang
From morn to evening, all the hot Fair-day,
So sweetly, that they stirred and haunted me
With a wild pleasure, falling on mine ear
Most like articulate sounds of things to come!
So gazed I, till the soothing things, I dreamt,
Lulled me to sleep, and sleep prolonged my dreams!
And so I brooded all the following morn,
Awed by the stern preceptor's face, mine eye
Fixed with mock study on my swimming book:
Save if the door half opened, and I snatched
A hasty glance, and still my heart leaped up,
For still I hoped to see the *stranger's* face,
Townsman, or aunt, or sister more beloved,
My playmate when we both were clothed alike!

Dear Babe, that sleepest cradled by my side,
Whose gentle breathings, heard in this deep calm,
Fill up the interspersèd vacancies
And momentary pauses of the thought!
My babe so beautiful! it thrills my heart
With tender gladness, thus to look at thee,
And think that thou shalt learn far other lore,
And in far other scenes! For I was reared
In the great city, pent 'mid cloisters dim,
And saw nought lovely but the sky and stars.
But *thou,* my babe! shalt wander like a breeze
By lakes and sandy shores, beneath the crags
Of ancient mountain, and beneath the clouds,
Which image in their bulk both lakes and shores
And mountain crags: so shalt thou see and hear

The lovely shapes and sounds intelligible
Of that eternal language, which thy God
Utters, who from eternity doth teach
Himself in all, and all things in himself.
Great universal Teacher! he shall mold
Thy spirit, and by giving make it ask.

    Therefore all seasons shall be sweet to thee,
Whether the summer clothe the general earth
With greenness, or the redbreast sit and sing
Betwixt the tufts of snow on the bare branch
Of mossy apple tree, while the nigh thatch
Smokes in the sun-thaw; whether the eave-drops fall
Heard only in the trances of the blast,
Or if the secret ministry of frost
Shall hang them up in silent icicles,
Quietly shining to the quiet Moon.

HART CRANE

UNITED STATES • 1899–1932

When I returned home to visit my parents last weekend, my dad's Aunt Edna came up in conversation. I asked for stories, photos. My dad returned to the kitchen with his mother's scrapbook. I was prepared to learn more about my history, not to see my father grow quiet and distant as he turned the pages. I realized that "over the greatness of such space" (the memories of my father), my "steps must be gentle." I also realized that the faces, voices, and music of our family's past will never be as strong for me as they are for him. I respect Crane for questioning his intrusion into the life of a woman who was not just a grandmother, but also his mother's mother, a woman named Elizabeth, who had a life before his. His ultimate realization—that perhaps there is some family history to which we have no rightful claim, which we cannot understand and in which we cannot share—is heartbreaking.

—Maggie Kenny, 27, Copywriter, Milwaukee, Wisconsin

My Grandmother's Love Letters

There are no stars to-night
But those of memory.
Yet how much room for memory there is
In the loose girdle of soft rain.

There is even room enough
For the letters of my mother's mother,
Elizabeth,
That have been pressed so long
Into a corner of the roof
That they are brown and soft,
And liable to melt as snow.

Over the greatness of such space
Steps must be gentle.
It is all hung by an invisible white hair.
It trembles as birch limbs webbing the air.

And I ask myself:

"Are your fingers long enough to play
Old keys that are but echoes:
Is the silence strong enough
To carry back the music to its source
And back to you again
As though to her?"
Yet I would lead my grandmother by the hand
Through much of what she would not understand;
And so I stumble. And the rain continues on the roof
With such a sound of gently pitying laughter.

RUBÉN DARÍO

NICARAGUA • 1867–1916

As a child I developed a great love for this poem. It is full of dreams.
—Marisa Salcines, 57, History Teacher, Miami, Florida

Story for Margarita

Margarita the sea is gleaming
and the breeze
brings the scent of lemon
and orange sprays,
and in my soul I feel a lark singing:
your voice.

Margarita, I'm going to tell you
a story.

        *   *   *

    Once there was a king who had
a herd of elephants,
a tent made of daylight,
a palace of diamonds,

a kiosk of malachite,
a robe of gold tissue
and a graceful daughter
so lovely,
Margarita,
as lovely as you.

    One afternoon the princess
looked up, and a new star shone.
She was mischievous,
and craved to get it down.

She wanted it for her breastpin,
to add to its décor,
with a poem and a pearl,
a feather and a flower.

Exquisite princesses
act a lot like you:
they cut roses and irises
and stars. Just like you.

So she went, the beautiful child,
under the sky and over the sea
to cut down the small white star
that had made her sigh.

She made her way upward
past the moon and farther;
with mischief, without permission
from her father.

When she left God's park
and returned that night,
she saw everything caught
in sweet, elegant light.

The king asked, "What have you done?
I looked all over—but you were lost!
And why are you blushing?
What's hiding there at your chest?

The princess didn't lie.
What she told the king was true:
"I went to cut my star
out of the giant blue."

The king cried, "Haven't I told you
the blue is not to be touched?
What foolishness! What fancy!
Child, you'll anger God!"

She said, "I didn't mean to.
I don't know why I went
to the star, to cut it down.
I rode on the waves and the wind."

Her father, angry now, said:
"You must go back to heaven.
Your punishment is to return
what you have stolen."

The princess felt deeply sad—
her precious flower of light!
Then the good Lord appeared,
smiling, at her side.

He said, "From my far fields,
I offer this rose—to keep.
Stars are the flowers of children
who dream of me when they sleep."

The king dressed in brilliant robes
and in a procession he
marched four hundred elephants
down to the shore of the sea.

The princess is beautiful—
and she still wears the star in the pin
that the poem, pearl, feather
and flower shine in.

*   *   *

Margarita, the sea is gleaming
and the breeze
brings the scent of lemon
and orange sprays:
your breath.

Child, now that you'll be far,
remember the princess and the star.

And remember the one
who told you a story.

Translated from the Spanish by Maggie Dietz

MARK DOTY

UNITED STATES • B. 1953

As a pediatrician, I learn a lot from children. This poem expresses how a child may have more insight about life than an adult might think.

—Seth Ammerman, 44, Pediatrician, San Francisco, California

Coastal

Cold April and the neighbor girl
   —our plumber's daughter—
      comes up the west street

from the harbor carrying,
   in a nest she's made
      of her pink parka,

a loon. *It's so sick,*
   she says when I ask.
      Foolish kid,

does she think she can keep
   this emissary of air?
      Is it trust or illness

that allows the head
   —sleek tulip—to bow
      on its bent stem

across her arm?
   Look at the steady,
      quiet eye. She is carrying

the bird back from indifference,
   from the coast
      of whatever rearrangement

the elements intend,
    and the loon allows her.
        She is going to call

the Center for Coastal Studies,
    and will swaddle the bird
        in her petal-bright coat

until they come.
    She cradles the wild form.
        Stubborn girl.

PAUL LAURENCE DUNBAR

UNITED STATES • 1872–1906

This is the first poem that I ever heard. My parents, both living, just cele-brated fifty years of marriage. They had only one child, and he had the plea-sure of hearing them read poetry to him even before, I imagine, he was able to speak. I wish that many more parents would read poetry to their chil-dren. It made a big difference for me; it's made a big difference for my chil-dren. I think it will make a huge difference for the children of America.

—Calvin Butts III, Pastor, Abyssinian Baptist Church, New York, New York

Little Brown Baby

Little brown baby wif spa'klin' eyes,
    Come to yo' pappy an' set on his knee.
What you been doin', suh—makin' san' pies?
    Look at dat bib—you's ez du'ty ez me.
Look at dat mouf—dat's merlasses, I bet;
    Come hyeah, Maria, an' wipe off his han's.
Bees gwine to ketch you an' eat you up yit,
    Bein' so sticky an' sweet—goodness lan's!

Little brown baby wif spa'klin' eyes,
    Who's pappy's darlin' an' who's pappy's chile?
Who is it all de day nevah once tries
    Fu' to be cross, er once loses dat smile?
Whah did you git dem teef? My, you's a scamp!
    Whah did dat dimple come f'om in yo' chin?
Pappy do' know you—I b'lieves you's a tramp;
    Mammy, dis hyeah's some ol' straggler got in!

Let's th'ow him outen de do' in de san',
    We do' want stragglers a-layin' 'roun' hyeah;
Let's gin him 'way to de big buggah-man;
    I know he's hidin' erroun' hyeah right neah.

Buggah-man, buggah-man, come in de do',
    Hyeah's a bad boy you kin have fu' to eat.
Mammy an' pappy do' want him no mo',
    Swaller him down f'om his haid to his feet!

Dah, now, I t'ought dat you'd hug me up close.
    Go back, ol' buggah, you sh'n't have dis boy.
He ain't no tramp, ner no straggler, of co'se;
    He's pappy's pa'dner an' playmate an' joy.
Come to you' pallet now—go to yo' res';
    Wisht you could allus know ease an' cleah skies;
Wisht you could stay jes' a chile on my breas'—
    Little brown baby wif spa'klin' eyes!

ROBERT FROST

UNITED STATES • 1874–1963

Robert Frost, New England's great poet, was born in California. The sonnet, written in couplets, recounts a childhood memory—standing with his father on the Pacific coast next to a thundering sea, he discerns in its blows and surges the rage of an angry God. "Put out the Light" comes from Shakespeare's Othello: *the words the title character speaks just before he smothers the sleeping Desdemona. Frost fearsomely reimagines Othello's awful turn on God's first command in Genesis.*

—M.D.

Once by the Pacific

The shattered water made a misty din.
Great waves looked over others coming in,
And thought of doing something to the shore
That water never did to land before.
The clouds were low and hairy in the skies,
Like locks blown forward in the gleam of eyes.
You could not tell, and yet it looked as if
The shore was lucky in being backed by cliff,
The cliff in being backed by continent;
It looked as if a night of dark intent
Was coming, and not only a night, an age.
Someone had better be prepared for rage.
There would be more than ocean-water broken
Before God's last *Put out the Light* was spoken.

LOUISE GLÜCK

UNITED STATES • B. 1943

Time

There was too much, always, then too little.
Childhood: sickness.
By the side of the bed I had a little bell—
at the other end of the bell, my mother.

Sickness, gray rain. The dogs slept through it. They slept on the bed,
at the end of it, and it seemed to me they understood
about childhood: best to remain unconscious.

The rain made gray slats on the windows.
I sat with my book, the little bell beside me.
Without hearing a voice, I apprenticed myself to a voice.
Without seeing any sign of the spirit, I determined
to live in the spirit.

The rain faded in and out.
Month after month, in the space of a day.
Things became dreams; dreams became things.

Then I was well; the bell went back to the cupboard.
The rain ended. The dogs stood at the door,
panting to go outside.

I was well, then I was an adult.
And time went on—it was like the rain,
so much, so much, as though it was a weight that couldn't be moved.

I was a child, half sleeping.
I was sick; I was protected.
And I lived in the world of the spirit,
the world of the gray rain,
the lost, the remembered.

Then suddenly the sun was shining.
And time went on, even when there was almost none left.
And the perceived became the remembered,
the remembered, the perceived.

THOMAS HARDY

ENGLAND • 1840–1928

At the Railway Station, Upway

"There is not much that I can do,
    For I've no money that's quite my own!"
    Spoke up the pitying child—
A little boy with a violin
At the station before the train came in,—
"But I can play my fiddle to you,
And a nice one 'tis, and good in tone!"

    The man in the handcuffs smiled;
The constable looked, and he smiled, too,
    As the fiddle began to twang;
And the man in the handcuffs suddenly sang
       With grimful glee:
    "This life so free
     Is the thing for me!"
And the constable smiled, and said no word,
As if unconscious of what he heard;
And so they went on till the train came in—
The convict, and boy with the violin.

The Self-Unseeing

Here is the ancient floor,
Footworn and hollowed and thin,
Here was the former door
Where the dead feet walked in.

She sat here in her chair,
Smiling into the fire;
He who played stood there,
Bowing it higher and higher.

Childlike, I danced in a dream;
Blessings emblazoned that day;
Everything glowed with a gleam;
Yet we were looking away!

SEAMUS HEANEY

IRELAND • B. 1939

My father was unequivocally an urban being, as am I. But still, and even before my father passed away, I found in this poem a masterly, deft, and poignant imagining of the dance of pride and shame that marks the relationship between father and adult son. Who, indeed, is following whom? Who is the originator, who the imitator? I never wanted to take up my father's occupation, but I found so much in his character and way of living immensely admirable. Could I separate the life from the work, and choose one while avoiding the other? Now that he has been gone for four years, I still haven't answered that.

—John Hildebidle, 54, Teacher, Cambridge, Massachusetts

Follower

My father worked with a horse-plough,
His shoulders globed like a full sail strung
Between the shafts and the furrow.
The horses strained at his clicking tongue.

An expert. He would set the wing
And fit the bright steel-pointed sock.
The sod rolled over without breaking.
At the headrig, with a single pluck

Of reins, the sweating team turned round
And back into the land. His eye
Narrowed and angled at the ground,
Mapping the furrow exactly.

I stumbled in his hobnailed wake,
Fell sometimes on the polished sod;
Sometimes he rode me on his back
Dipping and rising to his plod.

I wanted to grow up and plough,
To close one eye, stiffen my arm.
All I ever did was follow
In his broad shadow round the farm.

I was a nuisance, tripping, falling,
Yapping always. But today
It is my father who keeps stumbling
Behind me, and will not go away.

I was in a bad car accident when I was twenty, so my juvenile illusion of immortality was snatched away at a young age. Every time I read this poem the narrator's reflections on the inevitability of the eternal return and his powerlessness to stop it—the blackberries he would pick as a boy and suffer to get always ended up rotting—reminds me of how thin the thread of life is, in spite of our best efforts to strengthen it, and how vital it is to hold onto every moment of pleasure as long as we can.

—Mark Dowell, 25, Graduate Student (Hispanic Literature), Chapel Hill, North Carolina

Blackberry-Picking

For Philip Hobsbaum

Late August, given heavy rain and sun
For a full week, the blackberries would ripen.
At first, just one, a glossy purple clot
Among others, red, green, hard as a knot.
You ate that first one and its flesh was sweet
Like thickened wine: summer's blood was in it
Leaving stains upon the tongue and lust for
Picking. Then red ones inked up and that hunger
Sent us out with milk cans, pea tins, jam pots
Where briars scratched and wet grass bleached our boots.
Round hayfields, cornfields and potato drills

We trekked and picked until the cans were full,
Until the tinkling bottom had been covered
With green ones, and on top big dark blobs burned
Like a plate of eyes. Our hands were peppered
With thorn pricks, our palms sticky as Bluebeard's.

We hoarded the fresh berries in the byre.
But when the bath was filled we found a fur,
A rat-grey fungus, glutting on our cache.
The juice was stinking too. Once off the bush
The fruit fermented, the sweet flesh would turn sour.
I always felt like crying. It wasn't fair
That all the lovely canfuls smelt of rot.
Each year I hoped they'd keep, knew they would not.

GERARD MANLEY HOPKINS

ENGLAND • 1844–1889

It is a simple and glorious poem that not only gave me a glimpse of mortality at a very young age, but also a glimpse into the deeper, softer, and sadder side of my dad.

—Sarah VanWagenen Foxe, 24, Student/Mother, Sherman Oaks, California

It was like a strange flash, I was reciting this poem for the umpteenth time when all of a sudden I saw the scenery of my childhood: the old road on the way to the shopping center, my father driving me past a winery, the autumn trees shedding their leaves, the whole thing feeling so alien and remote, yet also very intimate. It was all so long ago. My mother was sick then. She is dead now, and so is my father.

—Michael Finberg, 40, Writer, Oakland, California

To read it in the morning is to lose the rest of the day.

—Patsy Davis, 58, Attorney, Washington, D.C.

Spring and Fall

To a Young Child

Márgarét, áre you gríeving
Over Goldengrove unleaving?
Leáves, líke the things of man, you
With your fresh thoughts care for, can you?
Áh! ás the heart grows older
It will come to such sights colder
By and by, nor spare a sigh
Though worlds of wanwood leafmeal lie;
And yet you *will* weep and know why.
Now no matter, child, the name:

Sórrow's spríngs áre the same.
Nor mouth had, no nor mind, expressed
What heart heard of, ghost guessed:
It ís the blight man was born for,
It is Margaret you mourn for.

HORACE

ROME • 65–8 B.C.E.

Ode I.9 / To Thaliarchus

See Mount Soracte shining in the snow.
See how the laboring overladen trees
Can scarcely bear their burdens any longer.

See how the streams are frozen in the cold.
Bring in the wood and light the fire and open
The fourth-year vintage wine in the Sabine jars.

O Thaliarchus, as for everything else,
Forget tomorrow. Leave it up to the gods.
Once the gods have decided, the winds at sea

Will quiet down, and the sea will quiet down,
And these cypresses and old ash trees will shake
In the storm no longer. Take everything as it comes.

Put down in your books as profit every new day
That Fortune allows you to have. While you're still young,
And while morose old age is far away,

There's love, there are parties, there's dancing and there's music,
There are young people out in the city squares together
As evening comes on, there are whispers of lovers, there's laughter.

Translated from the Latin by David Ferry

LANGSTON HUGHES

UNITED STATES • 1902–1967

My son, who was fourteen years old, gave me this poem twenty-five years ago. I was feeling very sad, my husband had passed away, and it inspired me to go on.

—Rita Campana, Sales Professional, Natick, Massachusetts

I memorized this poem when I was in the third grade, and I still remember it.

—Lauren Davis, 19, Student, Charlottesville, Virginia

If you have no dreams you have nothing to inspire you.

—Christopher V., 9, Student, Brooklyn, New York

I am planning to follow the poem's advice.

—Elysse Kremens, 11, Student, Montclair, New Jersey

Dreams

Hold fast to dreams
For if dreams die
Life is a broken-winged bird
That cannot fly.

Hold fast to dreams
For when dreams go
Life is a barren field
Frozen with snow.

JAMES JOYCE

IRELAND • 1882–1941

A Flower Given to My Daughter

Frail the white rose and frail are
Her hands that gave
Whose soul is sere and paler
Than time's wan wave.

Rosefrail and fair—yet frailest
A wonder wild
In gentle eyes thou veilest,
My blueveined child.

KENNETH KOCH

UNITED STATES • B. 1925

You Were Wearing

You were wearing your Edgar Allan Poe printed cotton blouse.
In each divided up square of the blouse was a picture of Edgar Allan
   Poe,
Your hair was blonde and you were cute. You asked me, "Do most
   boys think that most girls are bad?"
I smelled the mould of your seaside resort hotel bedroom on your hair
   held in place by a John Greenleaf Whittier clip.
"No," I said, "it's girls who think that boys are bad." Then we read
   Snowbound together
And ran around in an attic, so that a little of the blue enamel was
   scraped off my George Washington, Father of His Country, shoes.

Mother was walking in the living room, her Strauss Waltzes comb in
   her hair.
We waited for a time and then joined her, only to be served tea in
   cups painted with pictures of Herman Melville
As well as with illustrations from his book *Moby Dick* and from his
   novella, *Benito Cereno*.
Father came in wearing his Dick Tracy necktie: "How about a drink,
   everyone?"
I said, "Let's go outside a while." Then we went onto the porch and
   sat on the Abraham Lincoln swing.
You sat on the eyes, mouth, and beard part, and I sat on the knees.
In the yard across the street we saw a snowman holding a garbage can
   lid smashed into a likeness of the mad English king, George the
   Third.

YUSEF KOMUNYAKAA

UNITED STATES • B. 1947

The rhythm is hypnotic. The combination of innocence, sauciness, and childhood resilience is wonderful.

—Tammy Roberts, 39, Foster City, California

Venus's-flytraps

I am five,
    Wading out into deep
        Sunny grass,
Unmindful of snakes
    & yellowjackets, out
        To the yellow flowers
Quivering in sluggish heat.
    Don't mess with me
        'Cause I have my Lone Ranger
Six-shooter. I can hurt
    You with questions
        Like silver bullets.
The tall flowers in my dreams are
    Big as the First State Bank,
        & they eat all the people
Except the ones I love.
    They have women's names,
        With mouths like where
Babies come from. I am five.
    I'll dance for you
        If you close your eyes. No
Peeping through your fingers.
    I don't supposed to be
        This close to the tracks.

One afternoon I saw
      What a train did to a cow.
            Sometimes I stand so close
I can see the eyes
      Of men hiding in boxcars.
            Sometimes they wave
& holler for me to get back. I laugh
      When trains make the dogs
            Howl. Their ears hurt.
I also know bees
      Can't live without flowers.
            I wonder why Daddy
Calls Mama honey.
      All the bees in the world
            Live in little white houses
Except the ones in these flowers.
      All sticky & sweet inside.
            I wonder what death tastes like.
Sometimes I toss the butterflies
      Back into the air.
            I wish I knew why
The music in my head
      Makes me scared.
            But I know things
I don't supposed to know.
      I could start walking
            & never stop.
These yellow flowers
      Go on forever.
            Almost to Detroit.
Almost to the sea.
      My mama says I'm a mistake.
            That I made her a bad girl.
My playhouse is underneath
      Our house, & I hear people
            Telling each other secrets.

STANLEY KUNITZ

UNITED STATES • B. 1905

The Catch

It darted across the pond
toward our sunset perch,
weaving in, up, and around
a spindle of air,
this delicate engine
fired by impulse and glitter,
swift darning-needle,
gossamer dragon,
less image than thought,
and the thought come alive.
Swoosh went the net
with a practiced hand.
"Da-da, may I look too?"
You may look, child,
all you want.
This prize belongs to no one.
But you will pay all
your life for the privilege,
all your life.

D. H. LAWRENCE

ENGLAND • 1885–1930

The Piano

Somewhere beneath that piano's superb sleek black
Must hide my mother's piano, little and brown, with the back
That stood close to the wall, and the front's faded silk both torn,
And the keys with little hollows, that my mother's fingers had worn.

Softly, in the shadows, a woman is singing to me
Quietly, through the years I have crept back to see
A child sitting under the piano, in the boom of the shaking strings
Pressing the little poised feet of the mother who smiles as she sings.

The full throated woman has chosen a winning, living song
And surely the heart that is in me must belong
To the old Sunday evenings, when darkness wandered outside
And hymns gleamed on our warm lips, as we watched mother's fingers
    glide.

Or this is my sister at home in the old front room
Singing love's first surprised gladness, alone in the gloom.
She will start when she sees me, and blushing, spread out her hands
To cover my mouth's raillery, till I'm bound in her shame's heart-spun
    bands.

A woman is singing me a wild Hungarian air
And her arms, and her bosom, and the whole of her soul is bare,
And the great black piano is clamouring as my mother's never could
    clamour
And my mother's tunes are devoured of this music's ravaging glamour.

ABRAHAM LINCOLN

UNITED STATES • 1809–1865

It is unusual for a head of state to be a great writer, as Lincoln is in prose. And he has written a striking poem. The poem has sometimes been printed without the second part, the story of "Matthew" that begins "And here's an object more of dread." That shorter version, ending "I'm living in the tombs," is more conventional and less disturbing than this full version, with its nightmare of madness, the "sweet" funeral dirge of reason and the concluding phrase "I'm part of thee."

—R.P.

My Childhood-Home I See Again

My childhood-home I see again,
    And gladden with the view;
And still as mem'ries crowd my brain,
    There's sadness in it too.

O memory! thou mid-way world
    'Twixt Earth and Paradise,
Where things decayed, and loved ones lost
    In dreamy shadows rise.

And freed from all that's gross or vile,
    Seem hallowed, pure, and bright,
Like scenes in some enchanted isle,
    All bathed in liquid light.

As distant mountains please the eye,
    When twilight chases day—
As bugle-tones, that, passing by,
    In distance die away—

As leaving some grand water-fall
    We ling'ring, list its roar,

So memory will hallow all
    We've known, but know no more.

Now twenty years have passed away,
    Since here I bid farewell
To woods, and fields, and scenes of play
    And school-mates loved so well.

Where many were, how few remain
    Of old familiar things!
But seeing these to mind again
    The lost and absent brings.

The friends I left that parting day—
    How changed, as time has sped!
Young childhood grown, strong manhood grey,
    And half of all are dead.

I hear the lone survivors tell
    How nought from death could save,
Till every sound appears a knell,
    And every spot a grave.

I range the fields with pensive tread,
    And pace the hollow rooms;
And feel (companions of the dead)
    I'm living in the tombs.

And here's an object more of dread,
    Than ought the grave contains—
A human-form, with reason fled,
    While wretched life remains.

Poor Matthew! Once of genius bright,—
    A fortune-favored child—
Now locked for aye, in mental night,
    A haggard mad-man wild.

Poor Matthew! I have ne'er forgot
    When first with maddened will,

Yourself you maimed, your father fought,
  And mother strove to kill;

And terror spread, and neighbours ran,
  Your dang'rous strength to bind;
And soon a howling crazy man,
  Your limbs were fast confined.

How then you writhed and shrieked aloud,
  Your bones and sinnews bared;
And fiendish on the gaping crowd,
  With burning eye-balls glared.

And begged, and swore, and wept, and prayed,
  With maniac laughter joined—
How fearful are the signs displayed,
  By pangs that kill the mind!

And when at length, tho' drear and long,
  Time soothed your fiercer woes—
How plaintively your mournful song,
  Upon the still night rose.

I've heard it oft, as if I dreamed,
  Far-distant, sweet, and lone;
The funeral dirge it ever seemed
  Of reason dead and gone.

To drink its strains, I've stole away,
  All silently and still,
Ere yet the rising god of day
  Had streaked the Eastern hill.

Air held his breath; the trees all still
  Seemed sorr'wing angels round.
Their swelling tears in dew-drops fell
  Upon the list'ning ground.

But this is past, and nought remains
  That raised you o'er the brute.

Your mad'ning shrieks and soothing strains
    Are like forever mute.

Now fare thee well: more thou the cause
    Than subject now of woe.
All mental pangs, but time's kind laws,
    Hast lost the power to know.

And now away to seek some scene
    Less painful than the last—
With less of horror mingled in
    The present and the past.

The very spot where grew the bread
    That formed my bones, I see.
How strange, old field, on thee to tread,
    And feel I'm part of thee!

MARIANNE MOORE

UNITED STATES • 1887–1972

I first read this poem as a high school student. While I liked the familiarity of the Boston imagery—the glass flowers at Harvard, Longfellow's grave— I loved the language and the gravity of the final line. As I have grown older, the poem has begun to mean more to me. It has a kind of tension between science and philosophy, almost Taoist in a way.

—Leigh Montgomery, 28, Newspaper Researcher, Boston, Massachusetts

Silence

My father used to say,
"Superior people never make long visits,
have to be shown Longfellow's grave
or the glass flowers at Harvard.
Self-reliant like the cat—
that takes its prey to privacy,
the mouse's limp tail hanging like a shoelace from its mouth—
they sometimes enjoy solitude,
and can be robbed of speech
by speech which has delighted them.
The deepest feeling always shows itself in silence;
not in silence, but restraint."
Nor was he insincere in saying, "Make my house your inn."
Inns are not residences.

CAROL MUSKE

UNITED STATES • B. 1945

August, Los Angeles, Lullaby

The pure amnesia of her face,
newborn. I looked so far
into her that, for a while,

the visual held no memory.
Little by little, I returned
to myself, waking to nurse

those first nights in that
familiar room where all
the objects had been altered

imperceptibly: the gardenia
blooming in the dark
in the scarred water glass,

near the phone my handwriting
illegible, the patterned lamp-
shade angled downward and away

from the long mirror where
I stood and looked at
the woman holding her child.

Her face kept dissolving
into expressions resembling
my own, but the child's was pure

figurative, resembling no one.
We floated together in the space
a lullaby makes, head to head,

half-sleeping. *Save it,*
my mother would say, meaning
just the opposite. She didn't

want to hear my evidence
against her terrible optimism
for me. And though, despite her,

I can redeem, in a pawnshop
sense, almost any bad moment
from my childhood, I see now

what she must have intended
for me. I felt it for *her,*
watching her as she slept,

watching her suck as she
dreamed of sucking, lightheaded
with thirst as my blood flowed

suddenly into tissue that
changed it to milk. No matter
that we were alone, there's a

texture that moves between me
and whatever might have injured
us then. Like the curtain's sheer

opacity, it remains drawn
over what view we have of dawn
here in this onetime desert,

now green and replenished,
its perfect climate
unthreatened in memory—

though outside, as usual,
the wind blew, the bough bent,
under the eaves, the hummingbird

touched once the bloodcolored hourglass,
the feeder, then was gone.

OGDEN NASH

UNITED STATES • 1902–1971

I would not have been named Isabel without this poem. This is because my father sat up and said, "Our baby will be named Isabel." My mother thought of me—their brave, fast-thinking child. So I was named Isabel.

—Isabel Schneider, 8, Student, Rydal, Georgia

Adventures of Isabel

Isabel met an enormous bear,
Isabel, Isabel, didn't care;
The bear was hungry, the bear was ravenous,
The bear's big mouth was cruel and cavernous.
The bear said, Isabel, glad to meet you,
How do, Isabel, now I'll eat you!
Isabel, Isabel, didn't worry,
Isabel didn't scream or scurry.
She washed her hands and she straightened her hair up.
Then Isabel quietly ate the bear up.

Once in a night as black as pitch
Isabel met a wicked old witch.
The witch's face was cross and wrinkled,
The witch's gums with teeth were sprinkled.
Ho ho, Isabel! the old witch crowed,
I'll turn you into an ugly toad!
Isabel, Isabel, didn't worry,
Isabel didn't scream or scurry,
She showed no rage and she showed no rancor,
But she turned the witch into milk and drank her.

Isabel met a hideous giant,
Isabel continued self reliant.
The giant was hairy, the giant was horrid,
He had one eye in the middle of his forehead.

Good morning, Isabel, the giant said,
I'll grind your bones to make my bread.
Isabel, Isabel, didn't worry,
Isabel didn't scream or scurry.
She nibbled the zwieback that she always fed off,
And when it was gone, she cut the giant's head off.

Isabel met a troublesome doctor,
He punched and he poked till he really shocked her.
The doctor's talk was of coughs and chills
And the doctor's satchel bulged with pills.
The doctor said unto Isabel,
Swallow this, it will make you well.
Isabel, Isabel, didn't worry,
Isabel didn't scream or scurry.
She took those pills from the pill concocter,
And Isabel calmly cured the doctor.

FRANK O'HARA

UNITED STATES • 1926–1966

I was a grade school teacher many years ago and taught several children, shy and not aware of their gifts. This poem in its great simplicity tells the voyage of a lonely child . . . I smile each time I read it.

—Nita Donovan, 67, Retired Grade School Teacher, Pacific Palisades, California

Autobiographia Literaria

When I was a child
I played by myself in a
corner of the schoolyard
all alone.

I hated dolls and I
hated games, animals were
not friendly and birds
flew away.

If anyone was looking
for me I hid behind a
tree and cried out "I am
an orphan."

And here I am, the
center of all beauty!
writing these poems!
Imagine!

SYLVIA PLATH

UNITED STATES • 1932–1963

The first time I read this I was so impressed by the language (I had one of those ecstatic inhalations upon finishing the poem) that I read it out loud over and over and over, just to get the full effect.

—Alyson A., 16, Student, Springfield, Ohio

Alicante Lullaby

In Alicante they bowl the barrels
Bumblingly over the nubs of the cobbles
Past the yellow-paella eateries,
Below the ramshackle back-alley balconies,
    While the cocks and hens
    In the roofgardens
Scuttle repose with crowns and cackles.

Kumquat-colored trolleys ding as they trundle
Passengers under an indigo fizzle
Needling spumily down from the wires:
Alongside the sibilant harbor the lovers
    Hear loudspeakers boom
    From each neon-lit palm
Rumbas and sambas no ear-flaps can muffle.

O Cacophony, goddess of jazz and of quarrels,
Crack-throated mistress of bagpipes and cymbals,
Let be your *con brios,* your *capricciosos,*
Crescendos, cadenzas, prestos and *prestissimos,*
    My head on the pillow
    (*Piano, pianissimo*)
Lullayed by susurrous lyres and viols.

ARTHUR RIMBAUD

FRANCE • 1854–1891

The Lice Seekers

When the child's forehead full of red torments
Begs for the white swarm of indistinct dreams
There come close to his bed two big charming sisters
With frail fingers and silver nails.

They seat the child next to a window
Wide open, where blue air bathes a confusion of flowers
And in his heavy hair where the dew falls
Promenade their delicate fingers, terrible and enchanting.

He hears the singing of their timorous breath
Which bears the scent of long vegetable and rosy honeys
And which a whistling interrupts now and then, salivas
Taken back from the lip or desires for kisses.

He hears their black eyelashes beating beneath perfumed
Silences; and their fingers electric and sweet
Make crackle among his hazy indolences
Beneath their royal fingernails the death of little lice.

Now there is mounting in him the wine of Laziness,
Harmonica's sigh which could be delirious;
The child feels, according to the slowness of the caresses,
Spring up and die unceasingly a wish to cry.

Translated from the French by Kenneth Koch and Georges Guy

THEODORE ROETHKE

UNITED STATES • 1908–1963

Wouldn't everyone like to do something that would have everyone pointing up and shouting?

—Gerald Schwinn, 60, Consultant, Washington, D.C.

The kid on the greenhouse is wanting attention. But Theodore Roethke leaves you hanging. He doesn't tell you what happens after everyone is looking up at him.

—Jason Goodwin, 17, Student, Colfax, Indiana

Child on Top of a Greenhouse

The wind billowing out the seat of my britches,
My feet crackling splinters of glass and dried putty,
The half-grown chrysanthemums staring up like accusers,
Up through the streaked glass, flashing with sunlight,
A few white clouds all rushing eastward,
A line of elms plunging and tossing like horses,
And everyone, everyone pointing up and shouting!

ROBERT LOUIS STEVENSON

SCOTLAND • 1850–1894

I can remember being sick as a child. My dad bought me a drawbridge to play with while I was in bed. I loved driving the cars over the bridge and raising and lowering it. This poem brings that memory back to me every time I read it. It is a pleasant memory from that pleasant land of counterpane.

—Donna Herz, 48, Littleton, Colorado

This poem reminds me of myself when I was a little kid. When I was a little boy, I would always get sick. I would lie in bed and have nothing to do except play with my toy soldiers. This always kept me from being bored.

—Lance Tinkler, 15, Student, Miami, Florida

This poem has hypnotized me since I was small. There's a trance-like quality to calling the soldiers "leaden": it's the metal they are made of, but also how a fever makes you feel. And in the last four lines the change from "was" to "sees," past to present, is like leaving the real world for the eternal present of the imaginary world.

—R.P.

The Land of Counterpane

When I was sick and lay a-bed,
I had two pillows at my head,
And all my toys beside me lay
To keep me happy all the day.

And sometimes for an hour or so
I watched my leaden soldiers go,
With different uniforms and drills,
Among the bed-clothes, through the hills;

And sometimes sent my ships in fleets
All up and down among the sheets;
Or brought my trees and houses out,
And planted cities all about.

I was the giant great and still
That sits upon the pillow-hill,
And sees before him, dale and plain,
The pleasant land of counterpane.

WALT WHITMAN

UNITED STATES • 1819–1892

There Was a Child Went Forth

There was a child went forth every day,
And the first object he look'd upon, that object he became,
And that object became part of him for the day or a certain part of the
    day,
Or for many years or stretching cycles of years.

The early lilacs became part of this child,
And grass and white and red morning-glories, and white and red
    clover, and the song of the phoebe-bird,
And the Third-month lambs and the sow's pink-faint litter, and the
    mare's foal and the cow's calf,
And the noisy brood of the barnyard or by the mire of the pond-side,
And the fish suspending themselves so curiously below there, and the
    beautiful curious liquid,
And the water-plants with their graceful flat heads, all became part of
    him.

The field-sprouts of Fourth-month and Fifth-month became part of
    him,
Winter-grain sprouts and those of the light-yellow corn, and the
    esculent roots of the garden,
And the apple-trees cover'd with blossoms, and the fruit afterward,
    and wood-berries, and the commonest weeds by the road,
And the old drunkard staggering home from the outhouse of the
    tavern whence he had lately risen,
And the schoolmistress that pass'd on her way to the school,
And the friendly boys that pass'd, and the quarrelsome boys,

And the tidy and fresh-cheek'd girls, and the barefoot negro boy and
    girl,
And all the changes of city and country wherever he went.

His own parents, he that had father'd him and she that had conceiv'd
    him in her womb and birth'd him,
They gave this child more of themselves than that,
They gave him afterward every day, they became part of him.

The mother at home quietly placing the dishes on the supper-table,
The mother with mild words, clean her cap and gown, a wholesome
    odor falling off her person and clothes as she walks by,
The father, strong, self-sufficient, manly, mean, anger'd, unjust,
The blow, the quick loud word, the tight bargain, the crafty lure,
The family usages, the language, the company, the furniture, the
    yearning and swelling heart,
Affection that will not be gainsay'd, the sense of what is real, the
    thought if after all it should prove unreal,
The doubts of day-time and the doubts of night-time, the curious
    whether and how,
Whether that which appears so is so, or is it all flashes and specks?
Men and women crowding fast in the streets, if they are not flashes
    and specks what are they?
The streets themselves and the façades of houses, and goods in the
    windows,
Vehicles, teams, the heavy-plank'd wharves, the huge crossing at the
    ferries,
The village on the highland seen from afar at sunset, the river
    between,
Shadows, aureola and mist, light falling on roofs and gables of white
    or brown two miles off,
The schooner near by sleepily dropping down the tide, the little boat
    slacktow'd astern,
The hurrying tumbling waves quick-broken crests, slapping,
The strata of color'd clouds, the long bar of maroon-tint away solitary
    by itself, the spread of purity it lies motionless in,
The horizon's edge, the flying sea-crow, the fragrance of salt marsh
    and shore mud,

These became part of that child who went forth every day, and who
   now goes, and will always go forth every day.

On the Beach at Night

On the beach at night,
Stands a child with her father,
Watching the east, the autumn sky.

Up through the darkness,
While ravening clouds, the burial clouds, in black masses spreading,
Lower sullen and fast athwart and down the sky,
Amid a transparent clear belt of ether yet left in the east,
Ascends large and calm the lord-star Jupiter,
And nigh at hand, only a very little above,
Swim the delicate sisters the Pleiades.

From the beach the child holding the hand of her father,
Those burial-clouds that lower victorious soon to devour all,
Watching, silently weeps.

Weep not, child,
Weep not, my darling,
With these kisses let me remove your tears,
The ravening clouds shall not long be victorious,
They shall not long possess the sky, they devour the stars only in
   apparition,
Jupiter shall emerge, be patient, watch again another night, the
   Pleiades shall emerge,
They are immortal, all those stars both silvery and golden shall shine
   out again,
The great stars and the little ones shall shine out again, they endure,
The vast immortal suns and the long-enduring pensive moons shall
   again shine.

Then dearest child mournest thou only for Jupiter?
Considerest thou alone the burial of the stars?

Something there is,
(With my lips soothing thee, adding I whisper,
I give thee the first suggestion, the problem and indirection,)
Something there is more immortal even than the stars,
(Many the burials, many the days and nights, passing away,)
Something that shall endure longer even than lustrous Jupiter,
Longer than sun or any revolving satellite,
Or the radiant sisters the Pleiades.

WILLIAM CARLOS WILLIAMS

UNITED STATES • 1883–1963

The poet understood little boys. This is one of the best "commissioned" or assigned poems I know. And with the phrase "my Lord, you!" Williams acknowledges the tradition of poems commissioned by, or dedicated to, powerful Lords and Ladies.

—R.P.

The Turtle

(For My Grandson)

Not because of his eyes,
          the eyes of a bird,
                    but because he is beaked,
birdlike, to do an injury,
          has the turtle attracted you.
                    He is your only pet.
When we are together
          you talk of nothing else
                    ascribing all sorts
of murderous motives
          to his least action.
                    You ask me
to write a poem,
          should I have poems to write,
                    about a turtle.

The turtle lives in the mud
          but is not mud-like,
                    you can tell it by his eyes
which are clear,
          When he shall escape
                    his present confinement

he will stride about the world
        destroying all
                with his sharp beak.
Whatever opposes him
        in the streets of the city
                shall go down.
Cars will be overturned.
        And upon his back
                shall ride,
to his conquests,
        my Lord,
                you!

You shall be master!
        In the beginning
                there was a great tortoise
who supported the world.
        Upon him
                all ultimately
rests.
        Without him
                nothing will stand.
He is all wise
        and can outrun the hare.
                In the night
his eyes carry him
        to unknown places.
                He is your friend.

ANN WINTERS

UNITED STATES • B. 1939

At the turn in this unrhymed sonnet, addressed to a sleeping infant, the poet reveals that she is the mother above the cradle—"your mother" in the second line, becoming "I" in the seventh. The physical intimacy in the poem— soft light, close breathing—is balanced by the apparent remoteness of the mother's and child's worlds. I admire how this beautiful, familiar tension builds in the final lines, where the words "I know" separate the two, creating the mysterious space across which one loves while the other sleeps.
—M.D.

Night Light

Only your plastic night light dusts its pink
on the backs and undersides of things; your mother,
head resting on the nightside of one arm,
floats a hand above your cradle
to feel the humid tendril of your breathing.
Outside, the night rocks, murmurs . . . Crouched
in this eggshell light, I feel my heart
slowing, opened to your tiny flame

as if your blue irises mirrored me
as if your smile breathed and warmed
and curled in your face which is only asleep.
There is space between me, I know,
and you. I hang above you like a planet—
you're a planet, too. One planet loves the other.

WILLIAM BUTLER YEATS

IRELAND • 1865–1939

It was a poem my father often recited to me when I was a child. I was able to connect with my father only through literature, this poem affording us the illusion that we were a father and daughter performing a spectral chase scene in which I was the girl with apple blossoms in my hair, pursuing the ever-present horizon, and my father was the road-wearied philosopher.

—Acacia Carr, 17, Student, Santa Fe, New Mexico

The Song of Wandering Aengus

I went out to the hazel wood,
Because a fire was in my head,
And cut and peeled a hazel wand,
And hooked a berry to a thread;
And when white moths were on the wing,
And moth-like stars were flickering out,
I dropped the berry in a stream
And caught a little silver trout.

When I had laid it on the floor
I went to blow the fire aflame,
But something rustled on the floor,
And some one called me by my name:
It had become a glimmering girl
With apple blossom in her hair
Who called me by my name and ran
And faded through the brightening air.

Though I am old with wandering
Through hollow lands and hilly lands,
I will find out where she has gone,

And kiss her lips and take her hands;
And walk among long dappled grass,
And pluck till time and times are done
The silver apples of the moon,
The golden apples of the sun.

CHAPTER 2

EITHER WHOM TO LOVE OR HOW

JOHN ASHBERY

UNITED STATES • B. 1927

The poem begins and ends as a love poem, addressed to "you." But it also has meaning as a poem addressed to the reader, whom the poet courts and invites and wishes to see, and be seen by—like a lover. This ambiguity, like the smile that is both to the little world of "yourself" and to the larger world of "others" resembles the ambiguity of the "stars," with their names that somehow fit them: they can be the stars of astronomy, or of the movies.

—R.P.

Just Walking Around

What name do I have for you?
Certainly there is no name for you
In the sense that the stars have names
That somehow fit them. Just walking around,

An object of curiosity to some,
But you are too preoccupied
By the secret smudge in the back of your soul
To say much, and wander around,

Smiling to yourself and others.
It gets to be kind of lonely
But at the same time off-putting,
Counterproductive, as you realize once again

That the longest way is the most efficient way,
The one that looped among islands, and
You always seemed to be traveling in a circle.
And now that the end is near

The segments of the trip swing open like an orange.
There is light in there, and mystery and food.
Come see it. Come not for me but it.
But if I am still there, grant that we may see each other.

GEORGE BARKER

ENGLAND • 1913–1991

This poem is a letter written by a soldier on the battlefield to his mother. It shows that a love letter doesn't have to be written just to a young beautiful woman.

—Barbara Mackey, 58, Teacher, Adrian, Michigan

To My Mother

Most near, most dear, most loved and most far,
Under the window where I often found her
Sitting as huge as Asia, seismic with laughter,
Gin and chicken helpless in her Irish hand,
Irresistible as Rabelais, but most tender for
The lame dogs and hurt birds that surround her,—
She is a procession no one can follow after
But be like a little dog following a brass band.

She will not glance up at the bomber, or condescend
To drop her gin and scuttle to a cellar,
But lean on the mahogany table like a mountain
Whom only faith can move, and so I send
O all my faith and all my love to tell her
That she will move from mourning into morning.

BEI DAO

CHINA • B. 1949

The first time I read this poem—that very second—I just had to mail it to my best friend. It just really said it. She loved it, too. Now, every time I read this poem, and I read it quite a bit, I think of that absolute need I had to send it to her, and of the e-mail I got from her afterwards.

—Shelbie Spond, 20, Student, West Keansburg, New Jersey

A Bouquet

Between me and the world
You are a bay, a sail
The faithful ends of a rope
You are a fountain, a wind
A shrill childhood cry

Between me and the world
You are a picture frame, a window
A field covered with wild flowers
You are a breath, a bed
A night that keeps the stars company

Between me and the world
You are a calendar, a compass
A ray of light that slips through the gloom
You are a biographical sketch, a bookmark
A preface that comes at the end

Between me and the world
You are a gauze curtain, a mist
A lamp shining into my dreams
You are a bamboo flute, a song without words
A closed eyelid carved in stone

Between me and the world
You are a chasm, a pool
An abyss plunging down
You are a balustrade, a wall
A shield's eternal pattern

Translated from the Chinese by Bonnie S. McDougall

ELIZABETH BISHOP

UNITED STATES • 1911–1979

The Shampoo

The still explosions on the rocks,
the lichens, grow
by spreading, gray, concentric shocks.
They have arranged
to meet the rings around the moon, although
within our memories they have not changed.

And since the heavens will attend
as long on us,
you've been, dear friend,
precipitate and pragmatical;
and look what happens. For Time is
nothing if not amenable.

The shooting stars in your black hair
in bright formation
are flocking where,
so straight, so soon?
—Come, let me wash it in this big tin basin,
battered and shiny like the moon.

ELIZABETH BARRETT BROWNING

ENGLAND • 1806–1861

When I was ten years old, my mother decided to leave my father, taking my brother and me with her. I was devastated. A short time later, I discovered this sonnet tucked inside a book of poetry; my father had sent it to my mother. At that moment, I began to understand their pain, instead of focusing only on my own. It is the only poem I know by heart.

—Aimee Geoghan, 23, Student, Charleston, South Carolina

Go from me. Yet I feel that I shall stand

(*Sonnets from the Portuguese* 6)

Go from me. Yet I feel that I shall stand
Henceforward in thy shadow. Nevermore
Alone upon the threshold of my door
Of individual life, I shall command
The uses of my soul, nor lift my hand
Serenely in the sunshine as before,
Without the sense of that which I forbore, . .
Thy touch upon the palm. The widest land
Doom takes to part us, leaves thy heart in mine
With pulses that beat double. What I do
And what I dream include thee, as the wine
Must taste of its own grapes. And when I sue
God for myself, He hears that name of thine,
And sees within my eyes, the tears of two.

THOMAS CAMPION

ENGLAND • 1567–1620

A gorgeous, insightful description of an imaginary party. The verb "enlarge" makes the towers feel larger, as the "yellow waxen lights" and "honey love" make the great house or castle, where the party might take place, feel like a cozy, glowing beehive.

—R.P.

Now Winter Nights Enlarge

Now winter nights enlarge
The number of their hours,
And clouds their storms discharge
Upon the airy towers.
Let now the chimneys blaze
And cups o'erflow with wine;
Let well-tuned words amaze
With harmony divine!
Now yellow waxen lights
Shall wait on honey love
While youthful revels, masques and Courtly sights,
Sleep's leaden spells remove.

This time doth well dispense
With lovers' long discourse;
Much speech hath some defence,
Though beauty no remorse.
All do not all things well;
Some measures comely tread,
Some knotted riddles tell,
Some poems smoothly read.
The summer hath his joys,
And winter his delights;
Though love and all his pleasures are but toys,
They shorten tedious nights.

C. P. CAVAFY

GREECE • 1863–1933

The Bandaged Shoulder

He said he'd hurt himself against a wall or had fallen down.
But there was probably some other reason
for the wounded, the bandaged shoulder.

With a rather abrupt gesture,
reaching for a shelf to bring down
some photographs he wanted to look at,
the bandage came undone and a little blood ran.

I did it up again, taking my time
over the binding; he wasn't in pain
and I liked looking at the blood.
It was a thing of my love, that blood.

When he left, I found, in front of his chair,
a bloody rag, part of the dressing,
a rag to be thrown straight into the garbage;
and I put it to my lips
and kept it there a long while—
the blood of love against my lips.

Translated from the Greek by Edmund Keeley and Philip Sherrard

E. E. CUMMINGS

UNITED STATES • 1894–1962

I have read this poem so many times that the spine of the book is broken and always turns to its page. Today I gave that book away to the first person that I have ever truly and sincerely loved. I gave her the book because there is no gift I could give her that would be more honest. This poem has shaped who I am. It has been a long journey, but Cummings's poem set my heart on a course to find love, and I have arrived, only to truly understand the poem for the first time.

—Scott Nesbit, 18, Student, Powder Springs, Georgia

somewhere I have never travelled,gladly beyond

somewhere i have never travelled,gladly beyond
any experience,your eyes have their silence:
in your most frail gesture are things which enclose me,
or which i cannot touch because they are too near

your slightest look easily will unclose me
though i have closed myself as fingers,
you open always petal by petal myself as Spring opens
(touching skilfully,mysteriously)her first rose

or if your wish to close me,i and
my life will shut very beautifully,suddenly,
as when the heart of this flower imagines
the snow carefully everywhere descending;

nothing which we are to perceive in this world equals
the power of your intense fragility:whose texture
compels me with the colour of its countries,
rendering death and forever with each breathing

(i do not know what it is about you that closes
and opens;only something in me understands
the voice of your eyes is deeper than all roses)
nobody,not even the rain,has such small hands

EMILY DICKINSON

UNITED STATES • 1830–1886

It reminds me of someone dear to my heart, even when that person is not so close to me.

—Michael Forys, 19, Student, LaCrosse, Wisconsin

Wild Nights—Wild Nights! (249)

Wild Nights—Wild Nights!
Were I with thee
Wild Nights should be
Our luxury!

Futile—the Winds—
To a Heart in port—
Done with the Compass—
Done with the Chart!

Rowing in Eden—
Ah, the Sea!
Might I but moor—Tonight—
In Thee!

The whole thought of having a love but never being able to have it consumes me.

—Chelsea S., 16, Student, Burke, Virginia

Because of the uncertainty of life (and afterlife), love gains in intensity. This poem expresses the love I feel for my husband.

—Mary Cimarolli, 67, Richardson, Texas

If you were coming in the Fall (511)

If you were coming in the Fall,
I'd brush the Summer by
With half a smile, and half a spurn,
As Housewives do, a Fly.

If I could see you in a year,
I'd wind the months in balls—
And put them each in separate Drawers,
For fear the numbers fuse—

If only Centuries, delayed,
I'd count them on my Hand,
Subtracting, till my fingers dropped
Into Van Dieman's Land.

If certain, when this life was out—
That yours and mine, should be
I'd toss it yonder, like a Rind,
And take Eternity—

But, now, uncertain of the length
Of this, that is between,
It goads me, like the Goblin Bee—
That will not state—its sting.

JOHN DONNE

ENGLAND • 1572–1631

I like this poem because of its rhythm and it is a bit interesting, too, because I have no idea what it means. Like "get with child a mandrake root."

—Khristian S., 13, Student, Shiprock, New Mexico

It feels magic, like the words spoken by a hero who is about to go on a quest. It inspires me to look for magic in my life.

—Bridget Purcell, 18, Student, Rockville, Maryland

Song

Go and catch a falling star,
    Get with child a mandrake root,
Tell me where all past years are,
    Or who cleft the devil's foot,
Teach me to hear mermaids singing,
Or to keep off envy's stinging,
       And find
       What wind
Serves to advance an honest mind.

If thou be'st born to strange sights,
    Things invisible to see,
Ride ten thousand days and nights
    Till age snow white hairs on thee;
Thou, when thou return'st, wilt tell me
All strange wonders that befell thee,
       And swear
       Nowhere
Lives a woman true, and fair.

If thou find'st one, let me know;
    Such a pilgrimage were sweet—

Yet do not; I would not go,
    Though at next door we might meet.
Though she were true when you met her,
And last till you write your letter,
      Yet she
      Will be
False ere I come, to two or three.

MICHAEL DRAYTON

ENGLAND • 1563–1631

The insults are so inventive, so arresting, so extravagant, so celebrating of the loved one's power, that they amount to a cleverly disarming form of flattery.
—R.P.

Three sorts of serpents do resemble thee

(*Idea* 30)

Three sorts of serpents do resemble thee:
That dangerous eye-killing cockatrice,
The enchanting siren, which doth so entice,
The weeping crocodile—these vile pernicious three.
The basilisk his nature takes from thee,
Who for my life in secret wait dost lie,
And to my heart sendst poison from thine eye:
Thus do I feel the pain, the cause, yet cannot see.
Fair-maid no more, but Mer-maid be thy name,
Who with thy sweet alluring harmony
Hast played the thief, and stolen my heart from me,
And like a tyrant makst my grief thy game:
    Thou crocodile, who when thou hast me slain,
    Lamentst my death, with tears of thy disdain.

FAIZ AHMED FAIZ

PAKISTAN • 1911–1984

A very beautiful juxtaposition of romantic and realistic views of human existence.

—Malik Khan, 50, Engineer, Boxborough, Massachusetts

The Love I Gave You Once

My beloved,
My own,
Do not demand the love
I gave you once.

For a moment, I really believed
That you alone gave meaning
To my withered life;
That the accelerating pain
Of my unrequited love,
Would make me forget
All other torments
Of this troubled world;
That your face lent stability
To the restless spring;
That nothing else mattered
In this empty world
But your deep, seductive eyes.

For a moment, I really believed
That if I could only possess you,
I could conquer Fate itself.

But all that was false,
A mere illusion.

This world of ours bleeds
With more pains than just the pain of love;

And many more pleasures beckon us all the time
Than just the fleeting pleasure of a reunion with you.

For untold centuries,
The affluent have always woven many webs of intrigue,
Dark and cruel and mysterious,
And dressed them up in silks and brocades.
And for all those years,
On every street and in every bazaar,
Human bodies have been brazenly sold,
Dressed in dust and bathed in blood,
Malnourished, misshapen and baked by disease.

Time and time again,
My eyes are diverted
To this tragic scene,
Your beauty is alluring as ever,
Your arms inviting as always:
But how can I ever ignore
All this ugliness, all this pain?

Yes, my love,
This world of ours bleeds
With more pains than just the pain of love;
And many more pleasures beckon us all the time
Than just the fleeting pleasure of a reunion with you.

My beloved,
My own,
Do not demand the love
I gave you once.

Translated from the Arabic by Mahbub-ul-Haq

ROBERT FROST

UNITED STATES • 1874–1963

A great poem for reading aloud, for savoring the flow of the sentences as they sometimes rush past the rhymes, at other times stop for them.

—R.P.

To Earthward

Love at the lips was touch
As sweet as I could bear;
And once that seemed too much;
I lived on air

That crossed me from sweet things,
The flow of—was it musk
From hidden grapevine springs
Downhill at dusk?

I had the swirl and ache
From sprays of honeysuckle
That when they're gathered shake
Dew on the knuckle.

I craved strong sweets, but those
Seemed strong when I was young;
The petal of the rose
It was that stung.

Now no joy but lacks salt,
That is not dashed with pain
And weariness and fault;
I crave the stain

Of tears, the aftermark
Of almost too much love,
The sweet of bitter bark
And burning clove.

When stiff and sore and scarred
I take away my hand
From leaning on it hard
In grass and sand,

The hurt is not enough:
I long for weight and strength
To feel the earth as rough
To all my length.

I think that this is a love poem. I feel it is the true story of love.

—Juan S., 12, Student, Passaic, New Jersey

Dust of Snow

The way a crow
Shook down on me
The dust of snow
From a hemlock tree

Has given my heart
A change of mood
And saved some part
Of a day I had rued.

THOMAS HARDY

ENGLAND • 1840–1928

A Broken Appointment

You did not come,
And marching Time drew on and wore me numb.—
Yet less for loss of your dear presence there
Than that I thus found lacking in your make
That high compassion which can overbear
Reluctance for pure lovingkindness' sake
Grieved I, when, as the hope-hour stroked its sum,
You did not come.

You love not me,
And love alone can lend you loyalty;
—I know and knew it. But, unto the store
Of human deeds divine in all but name,
Was it not worth a little hour or more
To add yet this: Once, you, a woman, came
To soothe a time-torn man; even though it be
You love not me?

ROBERT HASS

UNITED STATES • B. 1941

If the poem is a consideration of perfect love, and the perhaps forever-hopeless pursuit of perfect love, then the difficulty of the ideal, and the "splendor" or straining toward it, are emphasized by the disorienting references to time. (Is it morning or evening? Are the two people embracing for minutes or weeks or months or years? How could it be years?)

—R.P.

Misery and Splendor

Summoned by conscious recollection, she
would be smiling, they might be in a kitchen talking,
before or after dinner. But they are in this other room,
the window has many small panes, and they are on a couch
embracing. He holds her as tightly
as he can, she buries herself in his body.
Morning, maybe it is evening, light
is flowing through the room. Outside,
the day is slowly succeeded by night,
succeeded by day. The process wobbles wildly
and accelerates: weeks, months, years. The light in the room
does not change, so it is plain what is happening.
They are trying to become one creature,
and something will not have it. They are tender
with each other, afraid
their brief, sharp cries will reconcile them to the moment
when they fall away again. So they rub against each other,
their mouths dry, then wet, then dry.
They feel themselves at the center of a powerful
and baffled will. They feel
they are an almost animal,
washed up on the shore of a world—
or huddled against the gate of a garden—
to which they can't admit they can never be admitted.

GEORGE HERBERT

ENGLAND • 1593–1633

In this astonishing conversation, the Love that speaks is God—though the poem has the intimate, deeply personal tone of a secular love lyric.
—M.D.

Love (III)

Love bade me welcome: yet my soul drew back,
    Guilty of dust and sin.
But quick-eyed Love, observing me grow slack
    From my first entrance in,
Drew nearer to me, sweetly questioning
    If I lacked any thing.

"A guest," I answered, "worthy to be here":
    Love said, "You shall be he."
"I, the unkind, ungrateful? Ah, my dear,
    I cannot look on thee."
Love took my hand, and smiling did reply,
    "Who made the eyes but I?"

"Truth, Lord; but I have marred them; let my shame
    Go where it doth deserve."
"And know you not," says Love, "who bore the blame?"
    "My dear, then I will serve."
"You must sit down," says Love, "and taste my meat."
    So I did sit and eat.

ROBERT HERRICK

ENGLAND • 1591–1674

The poem says it all.

—Jiri Kristek, Student, 21, Morrison, Colorado

To the Virgins, to Make Much of Time

Gather ye rosebuds while ye may,
    Old time is still a-flying;
And this same flower that smiles today
    Tomorrow will be dying.

The glorious lamp of heaven, the sun,
    The higher he's a-getting,
The sooner will his race be run,
    And nearer he's to setting.

That age is best which is the first,
    When youth and blood are warmer;
But being spent, the worse, and worst
    Times still succeed the former.

Then be not coy, but use your time,
    And, while ye may, go marry;
For, having lost but once your prime,
    You may forever tarry.

A. E. HOUSMAN

ENGLAND • 1859–1936

I like this poem because I can relate to it. Once I really liked this girl; I would have done anything for her, but that feeling went away as I got to know her better.

—Sohan B., 14, Student

Oh, when I was in love with you

(*A Shropshire Lad* 28)

Oh, when I was in love with you,
    Then I was clean and brave,
And miles around the wonder grew
    How well did I behave.

And now the fancy passes by,
    And nothing will remain,
And miles around they'll say that I
    Am quite myself again.

LANGSTON HUGHES

UNITED STATES • 1902–1967

This poem transmogrifies a broken heart into a work of art. What better use for a broken heart could there be?

—Alice Gordon, 49, Editor/Writer, New York, New York

While love is a great and beautiful thing, you needn't hurt yourself over it— even if it isn't returned in the way you expect it to be. I tend to get overly hung up on people I care about. I become paranoid and irrational, not able to think straight. When I read this poem, it gives a refreshing dose of reality.

—Terence Minerbrook, 17, Student, Brooklyn, New York

Life Is Fine

I went down to the river,
I set down on the bank.
I tried to think but couldn't,
So I jumped in and sank.

I came up once and hollered!
I came up twice and cried!
If that water hadn't a-been so cold
I might've sunk and died.

> *But it was*
> *Cold in that water!*
> *It was cold!*

I took the elevator
Sixteen floors above the ground.
I thought about my baby
And thought I would jump down.

I stood there and I hollered!
I stood there and I cried!

If it hadn't a-been so high
I might've jumped and died.

> *But it was*
> *High up there!*
> *It was high!*

So since I'm still here livin',
I guess I will live on.
I could've died for love—
But for livin' I was born.

Though you may hear me holler,
And you may see me cry—
I'll be dogged, sweet baby,
If you gonna see me die.

> *Life is fine!*
> *Fine as wine!*
> *Life is fine!*

BEN JONSON

ENGLAND • 1572–1637

Every time I read it I feel as if these words describe everything a man would feel for his perfect love. She seems untouchable, perfect, yet so real despite there being no reference to her in direct characteristics, but more to the feeling of her. It is that feeling placed into words that makes this poem so special and meaningful to me.

—Yinin Hu, 15, Student, Naperville, Illinois

His Excuse for Loving

Let it not your wonder move,
Less your laughter, that I love.
Though I now write fifty years,
I have had, and have, my peers.
Poets, though divine, are men;
Some have loved as old again.
And it is not always face,
Clothes, or fortune gives the grace,
Or the feature, or the youth;
But the language and the truth,
With the ardor and the passion,
Gives the lover weight and fashion.
If you then will read the story,
First, prepare you to be sorry
That you never knew till now
Either whom to love or how;
But be glad as soon with me
When you know that this is she
Of whose beauty it was sung,
She shall make the old man young,
Keep the middle age at stay,
And let nothing high decay,
Till she be the reason why
All the world for love may die.

In the seventeenth century a picture was no small thing, and Scotland (where I imagine the lady leaving the picture) no small distance from London. He makes his sentences and rhymes dance for the lady addressed, as though to shame her for ignoring such audible grace, distracted by visible defects.

—R.P.

My Picture Left in Scotland

I now think Love is rather deaf than blind,
    For else it could not be
        That she
Whom I adore so much should so slight me
    And cast my love behind;
I'm sure my language to her was as sweet,
        And every close did meet
      In sentence of as subtle feet,
       As hath the youngest he
    That sits in shadow of Apollo's tree.

O, but my conscious fears
      That fly my thoughts between,
     Tell me that she hath seen
   My hundreds of gray hairs,
   Told seven and forty years,
  Read so much waist as she cannot embrace
  My mountain belly and my rocky face;
And all these through her eyes have stopped her ears.

DENISE LEVERTOV

UNITED STATES • 1923–1997

Love Song

Your beauty, which I lost sight of once
for a long time, is long,
not symmetrical, and wears
the earth colors that make me see it.

A long beauty, what is that?
A song
that can be sung over and over,
long notes or long bones.

Love is a landscape the long mountains
define but don't
shut off from the
unseeable distance.

In fall, in fall,
your trees stretch
their long arms in sleeves
of earth-red and

sky-yellow. I take
long walks among them. The grapes
that need frost to ripen them

are amber and grow deep in the
hedge, half-concealed,
the way your beauty grows in long tendrils
half in darkness.

ANDREW MARVELL

ENGLAND · 1621–1678

The Definition of Love

My Love is of a birth as rare
As 'tis, for object, strange and high;
It was begotten by Despair
Upon Impossibility.

Magnanimous Despair alone
Could show me so divine a thing,
Where feeble Hope could ne'er have flown
But vainly flapped its tinsel wing.

And yet I quickly might arrive
Where my extended soul is fixed;
But Fate does iron wedges drive,
And always crowds itself betwixt.

For Fate with jealous eye does see
Two perfect loves, nor lets them close;
Their union would her ruin be,
And her tyrannic power depose.

And therefore her decrees of steel
Us as the distant poles have placed
(Though Love's whole world on us doth wheel),
Not by themselves to be embraced,

Unless the giddy heaven fall,
And earth some new convulsion tear,

And, us to join, the world should all
Be cramped into a planisphere.

As lines, so loves oblique may well
Themselves in every angle greet;
But ours, so truly parallel,
Though infinite, can never meet.

Therefore the love which us doth bind,
But Fate so enviously debars,
Is the conjunction of the mind,
And opposition of the stars.

GABRIELA MISTRAL

CHILE • 1889–1957

This poem appeals to me because I live through jealousy every day and I have to learn that it'll never go away.

—Lyndsey Gurowitz, 15, Student, North Miami, Florida

Ballad

He passed by with another;
I saw him pass by.
The wind ever sweet
and the path full of peace.
And these eyes of mine, wretched,
saw him pass by!

He goes loving another
over the earth in bloom.
The hawthorn is flowering
and a song wafts by.
He goes loving another
over the earth in bloom!

He kissed the other
by the shores of the sea.
The orange-blossom moon
skimmed over the waves.
And my heart's blood did not taint
the expanse of the sea!

He will go with another
through eternity.
Sweet skies will shine.
(God wills to keep silent.)
And he will go with another
through eternity!

Translated from the Spanish by Doris Dana

SUSAN MITCHELL

UNITED STATES • B. 1944

*This poem might be a variation on the theme "Be careful of your dreams,"
or perhaps it says something about integrity as a precondition to happiness.
Perhaps legend had it, among frogs, that if one could transform into a
prince and marry a princess, he'd have it made. Only after it happened to
one frog did he realize that if he wasn't true to his purpose in life, he'd never
find happiness. This poem is a splendid example of a human spirit dealing
creatively with the stuff that life throws at us.*

—Sara Baird, Lawyer, Phoenix, Arizona

From the Journals of the Frog Prince

In March I dreamed of mud,
sheets of mud over the ballroom chairs and table,
rainbow slicks of mud under the throne.
In April I saw mud of clouds and mud of sun.
Now in May I find excuses to linger in the kitchen
for wafts of silt and ale,
cinnamon and river bottom,
tender scallion and sour underlog.

At night I cannot sleep.
I am listening for the dribble of mud
climbing the stairs to our bedroom
as if a child in a wet bathing suit ran
up them in the dark.

Last night I said, "Face it, you're bored.
How many times can you live over
with the same excitement
that moment when the princess leans
into the well, her face a petal
falling to the surface of the water
as you rise like a bubble to her lips,

the golden ball bursting from your mouth?"
Remember how she hurled you against the wall,
your body cracking open,
skin shriveling to the bone,
the green pod of your heart splitting in two,
and her face imprinted with every moment
of your transformation?

I no longer tremble.

Night after night I lie beside her.
"Why is your forehead so cool and damp?" she asks.
Her breasts are soft and dry as flour.
The hand that brushes my head is feverish.
At her touch I long for wet leaves,
the slap of water against rocks.

"What are you thinking of?" she asks.
How can I tell her
I am thinking of the green skin
shoved like wet pants behind the Directoire desk?
Or tell her I am mortgaged to the hilt
of my sword, to the leek-green tip of my soul?
Someday I will drag her by her hair
to the river—and what? Drown her?
Show her the green flame of my self rising at her feet?
But there's no more violence in her
than in a fence or a gate.

"What are you thinking of?" she whispers.
I am staring into the garden.
I am watching the moon
wind its trail of golden slime around the oak,
over the stone basin of the fountain.
How can I tell her
I am thinking that transformations are not forever?

PABLO NERUDA

CHILE • 1904–1973

This poem was originally written in Spanish. In its translation, the poem's charm is lost a little, but not much. I like it because it demonstrates the feelings of a heartbroken lover who tries to forget his love; how he remembers the best moments with her and how he realizes they will not happen again. It is the way I have felt at times, wondering if feelings would ever come with someone else or never come back at all. It is a type of hope for people with broken hearts trying to kill their love to know they are not alone.

—Romina Bryce, 15, Student, Aventura, Florida

Tonight I Can Write

Tonight I can write the saddest lines.

Write, for example, "The night is starry
and the stars are blue and shiver in the distance."

The night wind revolves in the sky and sings.

Tonight I can write the saddest lines.
I loved her, and sometimes she loved me too.

Through nights like this one I held her in my arms.
I kissed her again and again under the endless sky.

She loved me, sometimes I loved her too.
How could one not have loved her great still eyes.

Tonight I can write the saddest lines.
To think that I do not have her. To feel that I have lost her.

To hear the immense night, still more immense without her.
And the verse falls to the soul like dew to the pasture.

What does it matter that my love could not keep her.
The night is starry and she is not with me.

This is all. In the distance someone is singing. In the distance.
My soul is not satisfied that it has lost her.

My sight tries to find her as though to bring her closer.
My heart looks for her, and she is not with me.

The same night whitening the same trees.
We, of that time, are no longer the same.

I no longer love her, that's certain, but how I loved her.
My voice tried to find the wind to touch her hearing.

Another's. She will be another's. As she was before my kisses.
Her voice, her bright body. Her infinite eyes.

I no longer love her, that's certain, but maybe I love her.
Love is so short, forgetting is so long.

Because through nights like this one I held her in my arms
my soul is not satisfied that it has lost her.

Though this be the last pain that she makes me suffer
and these the last verses that I write for her.

Translated from the Spanish by W. S. Merwin

FRANK O'HARA

UNITED STATES • 1926–1966

Everything in the poem is described from the point of view of someone in love, but, in the last five lines, O'Hara hits you right between the eyes with it.

—Esther Hurwitz, 41, Technical Writer, Ann Arbor, Michigan

Steps

How funny you are today New York
like Ginger Rogers in *Swingtime*
and St. Bridget's steeple leaning a little to the left

here I have just jumped out of a bed full of V-days
(I got tired of D-days) and blue you there still
accepts me foolish and free
all I want is a room up there
and you in it
and even the traffic halt so thick is a way
for people to rub up against each other
and when their surgical appliances lock
they stay together
for the rest of the day (what a day)
I go by to check a slide and I say
that painting's not so blue

where's Lana Turner
she's out eating
and Garbo's backstage at the Met
everyone's taking their coat off
so they can show a rib-cage to the rib-watchers
and the park's full of dancers with their tights and shoes
in little bags
who are often mistaken for worker-outers at the West Side Y
why not

the Pittsburgh Pirates shout because they won
and in a sense we're all winning
we're alive

the apartment was vacated by a gay couple
who moved to the country for fun
they moved a day too soon
even the stabbings are helping the population explosion
though in the wrong country
and all those liars have left the U N
the Seagram Building's no longer rivalled in interest
not that we need liquor (we just like it)

and the little box is out on the sidewalk
next to the delicatessen
so the old man can sit on it and drink beer
and get knocked off it by his wife later in the day
while the sun is still shining

oh god it's wonderful
to get out of bed
and drink too much coffee
and smoke too many cigarettes
and love you so much

SYLVIA PLATH

UNITED STATES • 1932–1963

"Love Letter" is about the end of a relationship, the stages a person goes through to move beyond it. The way you feel is all a matter of perspective, and I think the poem expresses that. The final realization that you can stand on your own two feet just as tall as when there's someone beside you has to be one of the best moments in a teenage girl's life.

—Kacey B., 14, Student, Miami Shores, Florida

Love Letter

Not easy to state the change you made.
If I'm alive now, then I was dead,
Though, like a stone, unbothered by it,
Staying put according to habit.
You didn't just toe me an inch, no—
Nor leave me to set my small bald eye
Skyward again, without hope, of course,
Of apprehending blueness, or stars.

That wasn't it. I slept, say: a snake
Masked among black rocks as a black rock
In the white hiatus of winter—
Like my neighbors, taking no pleasure
In the million perfectly-chiseled
Cheeks alighting each moment to melt
My cheek of basalt. They turned to tears,
Angels weeping over dull natures,
But didn't convince me. Those tears froze.
Each dead head had a visor of ice.

And I slept on like a bent finger.
The first thing I saw was sheer air
And the locked drops rising in a dew
Limpid as spirits. Many stones lay

Dense and expressionless round about.
I didn't know what to make of it.
I shone, mica-scaled, and unfolded
To pour myself out like a fluid
Among bird feet and the stems of plants.
I wasn't fooled. I knew you at once.

Tree and stone glittered, without shadows.
My finger-length grew lucent as glass.
I started to bud like a March twig:
An arm and a leg, an arm, a leg.
From stone to cloud, so I ascended.
Now I resemble a sort of god
Floating through the air in my soul-shift
Pure as a pane of ice. It's a gift.

EDGAR ALLAN POE

UNITED STATES • 1809–1849

It shows an almost unreachable beauty and affection. It reminds me of seeking a relationship, traveling from person to person in search of perfection. When found, a new piece of soul is found. But most of all it embodies the mythical stature and romance of my tender, tender age.

—Justin Bell, 18, Student, Derby, Kansas

To Helen

Helen, thy beauty is to me
    Like those Nicéan barks of yore,
That gently, o'er a perfumed sea,
    The weary, way-worn wanderer bore
    To his own native shore.

On desperate seas long wont to roam,
    Thy hyacinth hair, thy classic face,
Thy Naiad airs have brought me home
    To the glory that was Greece
And the grandeur that was Rome.

Lo! in yon brilliant window-niche
    How statue-like I see thee stand,
    The agate lamp within thy hand!
Ah! Psyche, from the regions which
    Are Holy Land!

CHRISTINA ROSSETTI

ENGLAND • 1830–1894

"No, Thank You, John"

I never said I loved you, John;
    Why will you tease me day by day,
And wax a weariness to think upon
        With always "do" and "pray"?

You know I never loved you, John;
    No fault of mine made me your toast:
Why will you haunt me with a face as wan
        As shows an hour-old ghost?

I dare say Meg or Moll would take
    Pity upon you, if you'd ask:
And pray don't remain single for my sake
        Who can't perform that task.

I have no heart?—Perhaps I have not;
    But then you're mad to take offence
That I don't give you what I have not got:
        Use your own common sense.

Let bygones be bygones:
    Don't call me false, who owed not to be true:
I'd rather answer "No" to fifty Johns
        Than answer "Yes" to you.

Let's mar our pleasant days no more,
    Song-birds of passage, days of youth:

Catch at to-day, forget the days before;
        I'll wink at your untruth.

Let us strike hands as hearty friends;
        No more, no less; and friendship's good:
Only don't keep in view ulterior ends,
        And points not understood

In open treaty. Rise above
        Quibbles and shuffling off and on.
Here's friendship for you if you like; but love,—
        No, thank you, John.

SAPPHO

GREECE • 612 B.C.E–?

At first the tranquility of Sappho's words struck me with their simple beauty, but as I read the poem over, the effect of the departed woman upon her friends reminded me of my own mother who passed away last spring. As my grief and tears subsided, I realized how much she was and is still a part of my life even though she is no longer present every day. I know she still watches everyone and takes care of them like she would have done if she were physically here.

—Anne Kristin T., 16, Student, North Miami Beach, Florida

To Atthis

My Atthis, although our dear Anaktoria
lives in distant Sardis,
she thinks of us constantly, and

of the life we shared in days when for her
you were a splendid goddess,
and your singing gave her deep joy.

Now she shines among Lydian women as
when the red-fingered moon
rises after sunset, erasing

stars around her, and pouring light equally
across the salt sea
and over densely flowered fields;

and lucent dew spreads on the earth to quicken
roses and fragile thyme
and the sweet-blooming honey-lotus.

Now while our darling wanders she thinks of
lovely Atthis's love,
and longing sinks deep in her breast.

She cries loudly for us to come! We hear,
for the night's many tongues
carry her cry across the sea.

Translated from the Greek by Willis Barnstone

WILLIAM SHAKESPEARE

ENGLAND • 1564–1616

Through contrasts of what love is not, Shakespeare gives you examples of what love is.

—Caitlin D., 14, Student, Odessa, Florida

Let me not to the marriage of true minds

(*Sonnets* 116)

Let me not to the marriage of true minds
Admit impediments. Love is not love
Which alters when it alteration finds,
Or bends with the remover to remove:
Oh, no! it is an ever-fixèd mark,
That looks on tempests and is never shaken;
It is the star to every wandering bark,
Whose worth's unknown, although his height be taken.
Love's not Time's fool, though rosy lips and cheeks
Within his bending sickle's compass come;
Love alters not with his brief hours and weeks,
But bears it out even to the edge of doom.
    If this be error and upon me proved,
    I never writ, nor no man ever loved.

SIR PHILIP SIDNEY

ENGLAND • 1554–1586

This simple yet extremely deep poem expresses how I felt about someone that I loved very dearly. He had my heart and I had his; together we were completed. I guess true love's feelings really do stand the test of time.

—Kim Nicholson, 20, Student, Philadelphia, Mississippi

My true love hath my heart and I have his

My true love hath my heart and I have his,
By just exchange one for another given;
I hold his dear, and mine he cannot miss,
There never was a better bargain driven.
    My true love hath my heart and I have his.

My heart in me keeps him and me in one,
My heart in him his thoughts and senses guides;
He loves my heart, for once it was his own,
I cherish his, because in me it bides.
    My true love hath my heart and I have his.

DEREK WALCOTT

ST. LUCIA, WEST INDIES • B. 1930

This poem is a joyful, and for me both comforting and inspiring, expression of accepting life's ultimate loneliness.

—Judith Segura, 52, Dallas, Texas

Love after Love

The time will come
when, with elation,
you will greet yourself arriving
at your own door, in your own mirror,
and each will smile at the other's welcome,

and say, sit here. Eat.
You will love again the stranger who was your self.
Give wine. Give bread. Give back your heart
to itself, to the stranger who has loved you

all your life, whom you ignored
for another, who knows you by heart.
Take down the love letters from the bookshelf,

the photographs, the desperate notes,
peel your own image from the mirror.
Sit. Feast on your life.

E. B. WHITE

UNITED STATES • 1899–1985

*It is a love poem that connects to the natural world. It is about spiders,
which I do not love, but respect. It is what I truly feel about my marriage—
a connection that can be both tenuous and strong.*

—Marguerite Cohen, 47, Physician, Portland, Oregon

Natural History

(A Letter to Katharine, from the King Edward Hotel, Toronto)

The spider, dropping down from twig,
Unwinds a thread of her devising:
A thin, premeditated rig
To use in rising.

And all the journey down through space,
In cool descent, and loyal-hearted,
She builds a ladder to the place
From which she started.

Thus I, gone forth, as spiders do,
In spider's web a truth discerning,
Attach one silken strand to you
For my returning.

WALT WHITMAN

UNITED STATES • 1819–1892

Because it speaks to friendship.

—Ed Santa Vicca, 52, Librarian, Phoenix, Arizona

I Saw in Louisiana a Live-Oak Growing

I saw in Louisiana a live-oak growing,
All alone stood it and the moss hung down from the branches,
Without any companion it grew there uttering joyous leaves of dark
    green,
And its look, rude, unbending, lusty, made me think of myself,
But I wonder'd how it could utter joyous leaves standing alone there
    without its friend near, for I knew I could not,
And I broke off a twig with a certain number of leaves upon it, and
    twined around it a little moss,
And brought it away, and I have placed it in sight in my room,
It is not needed to remind me as of my own dear friends,
(For I believe lately I think of little else than of them,)
Yet it remains to me a curious token, it makes me think of manly love;
For all that, and though the live-oak glistens there in Louisiana
    solitary in a wide flat space,
Uttering joyous leaves all its life without a friend a lover near,
I know very well I could not.

C. K. WILLIAMS

UNITED STATES • B. 1936

Still Life

All we do—how old are we? I must be twelve, she a little older;
     thirteen, fourteen—is hold hands
and wander out behind a barn, past a rusty hay rake, a half-collapsed
     old Model T,
then down across a barbed-wire gated pasture—early emerald
     ryegrass, sumac in the dip—
to where a brook, high with run-off from a morning storm,
     broadened and spilled over—
turgid, muddy, viscous, snagged here and there with shattered
     branches—in a bottom meadow.

I don't know then that the place, a mile from anywhere, and day,
     brilliant, sultry, balmy,
are intensifying everything I feel, but I know now that what made
     simply touching her
almost a consummation was as much the light, the sullen surge of
     water through the grass,
the coils of scent, half hers—the unfamiliar perspiration, talc,
     something else I'll never place—
and half the air's: mown hay somewhere, crushed clover underfoot,
     the brook, the breeze.

I breathe it still, that breeze, and, not knowing how I know for certain
     that it's that,
although it is, I know, exactly that, I drag it in and drive it—rich,
     delicious,

as biting as wet tin—down, my mind casting up flickers to fit it—
   another field, a hollow—
and now her face, even it, frail and fine, comes momentarily to focus,
   and her hand,
intricate and slim, the surprising firmness of her clasp, how
   judiciously it meshes mine.

All we do—how long does it last? an hour or two, not even one whole
   afternoon:
I'll never see her after that, and, strangely (strange even now), not
   mind, as though,
in that afternoon the revelations weren't only of the promises of flesh,
   but of resignation—
all we do is trail along beside the stream until it narrows, find the one-
   log bridge
and cross into the forest on the other side: silent footfalls, hills, a crest,
   a lip.

I don't know then how much someday—today—I'll need it all, how
   much want to hold it,
and, not knowing why, not knowing still how time can tempt us so
   emphatically and yet elude us,
not have it, not the way I would, not the way I want to have *that* day,
   that light,
the motes that would have risen from the stack of straw we leaned on
   for a moment,
the tempered warmth of air which so precisely seemed the coefficient
   of my fearful ardor,

not, after all, even the objective place, those shifting paths I can't
   really follow now
but only can compile from how many other ambles into other woods,
   other stoppings in a glade—
(for a while we were lost, and frightened; night was just beyond the
   hills; we circled back)—
even, too, her gaze, so darkly penetrating, then lifting idly past, is so
   much imagination,
a portion of that figured veil we cast against oblivion, then try, with
   little hope, to tear away.

WILLIAM CARLOS WILLIAMS

UNITED STATES • 1883–1963

This poem is one of my favorites because it is so clear and well put. It's not just talking about roses. The poem manages to capture the struggle between cynicism and a retained enthusiasm and appreciation of life, however brief life may be. The poem takes this idea, which I could babble confusedly about for hours and hours, and tells it neatly in a simple handful of lines.

—Lindsey Ward, 17, Student, Brooklyn, New York

The Act

There were the roses, in the rain.
Don't cut them, I pleaded.
    They won't last, she said.
But they're so beautiful
    where they are.
Agh, we were all beautiful once, she
    said,
and cut them and gave them to me
    in my hand.

WILLIAM BUTLER YEATS

IRELAND • 1865–1939

This poem sings to me. I find it as richly embroidered as the cloths of which it speaks.

—Eliza Shin, 28, Resident Physician, St. Louis, Missouri

It is impossible not to be touched by it.

—Grainne Blessing, 19, Student

He Wishes for the Cloths of Heaven

Had I the heavens' embroidered cloths,
Enwrought with golden and silver light,
The blue and the dim and the dark cloths
Of night and light and the half-light,
I would spread the cloths under your feet:
But I, being poor, have only my dreams;
I have spread my dreams under your feet;
Tread softly because you tread on my dreams.

CHAPTER 3

THE FORGETFUL
KINGDOM OF DEATH

STERLING A. BROWN

UNITED STATES • 1901–1989

Thoughts of Death

Thoughts of death
Crowd over my happiness
Like dark clouds
Over the silver sickle of the moon.

> *Death comes to some*
> *Like a grizzled gangster*
> *Clubbing in the night;*
> *To some*
> *Like an obstinate captain*
> *Steadily besieging barriers;*
> *To some like a brown adder*
> *Lurking in violet-speckled underbrush;*
> *To some*
> *Like a gentle nurse*
> *Taking their toys and stroking their hot brows.*
>
> *Death will come to you, I think,*
> *Like an old shrewd gardener*
> *Culling his rarest blossom. . . .*

GEOFFREY CHAUCER

ENGLAND • CA. 1343–1400

I love to say these lines aloud, though my pronunciation of Middle English is clumsy. Words that look foreign in print—like "a-goon" and "noldest"— change in the mouth, within Chaucer's spare interweaving of admiration and grief.

—M.D.

I have of sorwe so grete woon

I have of sorwe so grete woon
That joye gete I never noon
Now that I see my lady bright
Which I have loved with al my myght
Is fro me deed and is a-goon.

Allas, Deeth, what ayleth thee
That thou noldest have taken me
Whan thou toke my lady sweete
That was so fayr, so fresh, so fre,
So good, that men may wel se
Of al goodnesse she had no meete.

FRANCES CORNFORD

ENGLAND • 1886–1960

The Watch

I wakened on my hot, hard bed,
Upon the pillow lay my head;
Beneath the pillow I could hear
My little watch was ticking clear.
I thought the throbbing of it went
Like my continual discontent;
I thought it said in every tick:
I am so sick, so sick, so sick;
O death, come quick, come quick, come quick,
Come quick, come quick, come quick, come quick.

EMILY DICKINSON

UNITED STATES • 1830–1886

I say it every night, as a kind of prayer, just before I go to sleep. It seems a good reminder of life's whole pattern.

—Doris Abramson, 75, Retired Professor (Theater), New Salem, Massachusetts

The Heart asks Pleasure—first— (536)

The Heart asks Pleasure—first—
And then—Excuse from Pain—
And then—those little Anodynes
That deaden suffering—

And then—to go to sleep—
And then—if it should be
The will of its Inquisitor
The privilege to die—

I heard a Fly buzz—when I died— (465)

I heard a Fly buzz—when I died—
The Stillness in the Room
Was like the Stillness in the Air—
Between the Heaves of Storm—

The Eyes around—had wrung them dry—
And Breaths were gathering firm
For that last Onset—when the King
Be witnessed—in the Room—

I willed my Keepsakes—Signed away
What portion of me be
Assignable—and then it was
There interposed a Fly—

With Blue—uncertain stumbling Buzz—
Between the light—and me—
And then the Windows failed—and then
I could not see to see—

JOHN DONNE

ENGLAND • 1572–1631

About five years ago, my father introduced me to this poem, and it was the first poem I memorized.

—Stephanie T., 17, Student, Oakhurst, New Jersey

In eloquent and brief form Donne shows life, death are separated only by a comma, a breath—and the spirit, or life everlasting, lives on. I fell in love with Donne in high school. Now the poem has deep significance for me. I am forty-eight years old and in my fifth year of Lou Gehrig's disease (ALS, amyotrophic lateral sclerosis), a degenerative neuromuscular disease for which there's no cure, with a three-to-five-year average life expectancy. I was a competitive runner and lawyer; now I'm in a wheelchair and can barely speak. I use a computer to talk, similar to that used by the physicist, Stephen Hawking, who has ALS. Like many who are living with dying (as we all are, of course), I am grateful for each day. I have a wonderful life, a wonderful family—daughter, high school senior, and husband—and fabulous friends.

—Laura Murphy, 48, Atlanta, Georgia

Death, be not proud, though some have callèd thee

(*Holy Sonnets* 10)

Death, be not proud, though some have callèd thee
Mighty and dreadful, for thou art not so;
For those whom thou think'st thou dost overthrow
Die not, poor Death; nor yet canst thou kill me.
From rest and sleep, which but thy pictures be,
Much pleasure; then, from thee much more must flow,
And soonest our best men with thee do go,
Rest of their bones and soul's delivery.
Thou art slave to fate, chance, kings, and desperate men,
And dost with poison, war, and sickness dwell;

And poppy or charms can make us sleep as well,
And better than thy stroke. Why swell'st thou then?
One short sleep passed, we wake eternally,
And death shall be no more. Death, thou shalt die.

LINDA GREGG

UNITED STATES • B. 1942

Impatient with elegy, with "weakness," with all the conventional terms of grief and pain, with the darkness that is "easy," mourning the death of a six-year-old child, the poet resolves her poem with an image—and an image of a perhaps-consoling darkness.

—R.P.

The Poet Goes about Her Business

For Michele (1966–1972)

Michele has become another dead little girl. An easy poem.
Instant Praxitelean. Instant seventy-five year old photograph
of my grandmother when she was a young woman with shadows
I imagine were blue around her eyes. The beauty of it.
Such guarded sweetness. What a greed of bruised gardenias.
Oh Christ, whose name rips silk, I have seen raw cypresses
so dark the mind comes to them without color.
Dark on the Greek hillside. Dark, volcanic, dry and stone.
Where the oldest women of the world are standing dressed in black
up in the branches of fig trees in the gorge
knocking with as much quickness as their weakness will allow.
Weakness which my heart must not confuse with tenderness.
And on the other side of the island a woman
walks up the path with a burden of leaves on her head,
guiding the goats with sounds she makes up,
and then makes up again. The other darkness is easy:
the men in the dreams who come in together to me with knives.
There are so many traps, and many look courageous.
The body goes into such raptures of obedience.
But the huge stones on the desert resemble
nobody's mother. I remember the snake.
After its skin had been cut away, and it was dropped

it started to move across the clearing.
Making its beautiful waving motion.
It was all meat and bone. Pretty soon it was covered with dust.
It seemed to know exactly where it wanted to go.
Toward any dark trees.

FULKE GREVILLE, LORD BROOKE

ENGLAND • 1554–1628

You that seek what life is in death

(*Caelica* 82)

You that seek what life is in death,
Now find it air that once was breath.
New names unknown, old names gone:
Till time end bodies, but souls none.
    Reader! then make time, while you be,
    But steps to your eternity.

GEORGE HERBERT

ENGLAND • 1593–1633

Death

Death, thou wast once an uncouth hideous thing,
            Nothing but bones,
   The sad effect of sadder groans:
Thy mouth was open, but thou couldst not sing.

For we considered thee as at some six
            Or ten years hence,
   After the loss of life and sense,
Flesh being turned to dust, and bones to sticks.

We looked on this side of thee, shooting short;
            Where we did find
   The shells of fledge souls left behind,
Dry dust, which sheds no tears, but may extort.

But since our Savior's death did put some blood
            Into thy face,
   Thou art grown fair and full of grace,
Much in request, much sought for as a good.

For we do now behold thee gay and glad,
            As at Doomsday;
   When souls shall wear their new array,
And all thy bones with beauty shall be clad.

Therefore we can go die as sleep, and trust
            Half that we have
   Unto an honest faithful grave;
Making our pillows either down, or dust.

ROBERT HERRICK

ENGLAND • 1591–1674

This poem is important to me because it reminds me of life. Like a daffodil we grow from a seed, bit by bit, some leaves form, and the stem starts to grow. Then comes the bud, the time in your life when your personality starts to bloom. Then your middle-aged years come along and your real life starts. As you grow older your petals start to fall, and your stem turns to brown. You eventually die and are missed. Many others long to have you come back. Then as spring comes along again, a new person or daffodil is born. You never know what you have lost until it's gone.

—McKenna K., 13, Student, Sumner, Washington

To Daffodils

Fair Daffodils, we weep to see
    You haste away so soon:
As yet the early-rising sun
    Has not attained his noon.
        Stay, stay,
    Until the hasting day
           Has run
    But to the evensong;
And, having prayed together, we
      Will go with you along.

We have short time to stay, as you;
    We have as short a spring;
As quick a growth to meet decay,
    As you, or anything.
        We die,
    As your hours do, and dry
           Away,
    Like to the summer's rain;
Or as the pearls of morning's dew
      Ne'er to be found again.

A. E. HOUSMAN

ENGLAND • 1859–1936

It helped me cope with the mental illness of my older brother who had been a star athlete, a very talented individual. I used this poem to keep the brother of my childhood alive to me, to accept the loss and celebrate what he had been and still was, somewhere inside.

—Eleanor Wormwood, 50, Colton Point, Maryland

We are not immortal and we may not be remembered. It's a beautiful poem.

—Gillian H., 15, Student, Westfield, New Jersey

To an Athlete Dying Young

The time you won your town the race
We chaired you through the market-place;
Man and boy stood cheering by,
And home we brought you shoulder-high.

Today, the road all runners come,
Shoulder-high we bring you home,
And set you at your threshold down,
Townsman of a stiller town.

Smart lad, to slip betimes away
From fields where glory does not stay
And early though the laurel grows
It withers quicker than the rose.

Now you will not swell the rout
Of lads that wore their honors out,
Runners whom renown outran
And the name died before the man.

So set, before its echoes fade,
The fleet foot on the sill of shade,

And hold to the low lintel up
The still-defended challenge-cup.

And round that early-laureled head
Will flock to gaze the strengthless dead,
And find unwithered on its curls
The garland briefer than a girl's.

RANDALL JARRELL

UNITED STATES • 1914–1965

Like any mother, I've always been aware of the horror of war, the unspeakable expendability of our youth. My son did not go to Vietnam due to severe asthma. It was the only time I blessed the ailment. But on many occasions I have recited this poem.

—Pearl Stein Selinsky, 70, Retired Teacher, Sacramento, California

As a child I couldn't understand why the movie newsreels and, later, television, showed jubilant Americans waving the boys off to war. It troubled and puzzled me for years. Later, my father explained that people did not realize the horrors of war. In just five lines Jarrell captures those horrors for me. I only learned of the poem a few years ago at age fifty-three, and enthusiasm for war still puzzles me.

—Joanne Dobrenski, 55, Retired, Mechanicsburg, Pennsylvania

In five lines, the poet drew pictures for the ten-year-old that I was about the horror, the futility, the senselessness, the bloodiness, and the ambiguity of war.

—Cynthia Bellows, 45, Employment and Training Specialist, Jonesboro, Maine

The Death of the Ball Turret Gunner

From my mother's sleep I fell into the State,
And I hunched in its belly till my wet fur froze.
Six miles from earth, loosed from its dream of life,
I woke to black flak and the nightmare fighters.
When I died they washed me out of the turret with a hose.

HENRY KING

ENGLAND • 1592–1669

A Contemplation upon Flowers

Brave flowers, that I could gallant it like you
And be as little vain;
You come abroad, and make a harmless show,
And to your beds of earth again;
You are not proud, you know your birth
For your embroidered garments are from earth.

You do obey your months and times, but I
Would have it ever spring;
My fate would know no winter, never die
Nor think of such a thing;
Oh, that I could my bed of earth but view
And smile, and look as cheerfully as you.

Oh, teach me to see death and not to fear,
But rather to take truce;
How often have I seen you at a bier,
And there look fresh and spruce;
You fragrant flowers then teach me that my breath
Like yours may sweeten, and perfume my death.

MARY KINZIE

UNITED STATES • B. 1944

After the powerful description of the shop girls' fettersome clothing, their stumbling in the rain-soaked field, the line "Here that girl ran last, so long ago, to be run through" strikes across the page like lightning, transforming what comes before it.

—M.D.

The Bolt

That girl so long ago walked, as they all did, shop girls,
Little cousins, and church friends, to the unflattering
Hack of the hem just where the calf begins to swell,
Felt ruchings of the bodice's stiff panels
Gall the flesh beside the flattening ornate
Armature of underwear (like pads and straps
For livestock, fretted by tooling and bright studs),
So she must yank her knees against
Pounds of rigid drapery in the storm of heat,

Trailing through the pestering, gray heads
Of Queen Anne's lace, wind ravelling
Her hair and sweeping through prolific
Jagged-bladed grass—a wind that pressed down
There like God with both His hands, mashing the air,
Darkening the hole where the dry mouth of the wood
Yawned to drink the stumbling travelers already touched
By the heavy sacs of rain that broke and ran
In gouts down saturated pleats of serge . . .

Here that girl ran last, so long ago, to be run through
By one long lightning thread that entered, through
A slender purple bruise, the creamy skin of her temple.

The instant that it happened, nobody remembered
How she looked or spoke, so quickly had she blended
With this evocation of her having been.

This was the past: a stroke of imagery stare-
Frozen, finished in suspension.

WALTER SAVAGE LANDOR

ENGLAND • 1775–1864

Some poets were inspecting an actual hair of the famous, terrifying, glamorous Borgia—one of them had swiped the hair from a museum—and Landor wrote this poem about the sight. The poem has been published both with "unfold" and "enfold" at the end of the third line, and both words work, with their implications of disclosing and enclosing.

—R.P.

On Seeing a Hair of Lucretia Borgia

Borgia, thou once wert almost too august
And high for adoration; now thou'rt dust.
All that remains of thee these plaits unfold,
Calm hair, meandering in pellucid gold.

JOHN CROWE RANSOM

UNITED STATES • 1888–1974

Janet Waking

Beautifully Janet slept
Till it was deeply morning. She woke then
And thought about her dainty-feathered hen,
To see how it had kept.

One kiss she gave her mother.
Only a small one gave she to her daddy
Who would have kissed each curl of his shining baby;
No kiss at all for her brother.

"Old Chucky, old Chucky!" she cried,
Running across the world upon the grass
To Chucky's house, and listening. But alas,
Her Chucky had died.

It was a transmogrifying bee
Came droning down on Chucky's old bald head
And sat and put the poison. It scarcely bled,
But how exceedingly

And purply did the knot
Swell with the venom and communicate
Its rigor! Now the poor comb stood up straight
But Chucky did not.

So there was Janet
Kneeling on the wet grass, crying her brown hen
(Translated far beyond the daughters of men)
To rise and walk upon it.

And weeping fast as she had breath
Janet implored us, "Wake her from her sleep!"
And would not be instructed in how deep
Was the forgetful kingdom of death.

THEODORE ROETHKE

UNITED STATES • 1908–1963

Elegy for Jane

My Student, Thrown by a Horse

I remember the neckcurls, limp and damp as tendrils;
And her quick look, a sidelong pickerel smile;
And how, once startled into talk, the light syllables leaped for her,
And she balanced in the delight of her thought,
A wren, happy, tail into the wind,
Her song trembling the twigs and small branches.
The shade sang with her;
The leaves, their whispers turned to kissing;
And the mold sang in the bleached valleys under the rose.

Oh, when she was sad, she cast herself down into such a pure depth,
Even a father could not find her:
Scraping her cheek against straw;
Stirring the clearest water.
My sparrow, you are not here,
Waiting like a fern, making a spiny shadow.
The sides of wet stones cannot console me,
Nor the moss, wound with the last light.

If only I could nudge you from this sleep,
My maimed darling, my skittery pigeon.
Over this damp grave I speak the words of my love:
I, with no rights in this matter,
Neither father nor lover.

WILLIAM SHAKESPEARE

ENGLAND • 1564–1616

Fear no more the heat o' the sun

Fear no more the heat o' the sun,
    Nor the furious winter's rages;
Thou thy worldly task hast done,
    Home art gone, and ta'en thy wages:
Golden lads and girls all must,
As chimney-sweepers, come to dust.

Fear no more the frown o' the great;
    Thou art past the tyrant's stroke;
Care no more to clothe and eat;
    To thee the reed is as the oak:
The scepter, learning, physic, must
All follow this, and come to dust.

Fear no more the lightning flash,
    Nor the all-dreaded thunder stone;
Fear not slander, censure rash;
    Thou hast finished joy and moan:
All lovers young, all lovers must
Consign to thee, and come to dust.

No exorciser harm thee!
Nor no witchcraft charm thee!
Ghost unlaid forbear thee!
Nothing ill come near thee!
Quiet consummation have;
And renownèd be thy grave!

MAY SWENSON

UNITED STATES • 1919–1989

What I seem to need, over and over again, from this poem, is its seeming naïveté (the hobby-horse, nursery-rhyme canter, the child-simple diction and rhyme) as it grapples with the unthinkable.

—Polly Robertus, 51, Editor/Writer, Austin, Texas

Question

Body my house
my horse my hound
what will I do
when you are fallen

Where will I sleep
How will I ride
What will I hunt

Where can I go
without my mount
all eager and quick
How will I know
in thicket ahead
is danger or treasure
when Body my good
bright dog is dead

How will it be
to lie in the sky
without roof or door
and wind for an eye

With cloud for shift
how will I hide?

DYLAN THOMAS

WALES • 1914–1953

I've lost many people who were very close and dear to me in my life. This poem is my way of comforting myself and saying a prayer for the souls of those who have left this world. Even though death might be able to kill and break faith and create doubt, there is more than just death.

—Jade Stamatien, 18, Student, Worcester, Massachusetts

Such insolence. Such triumph. And such loneliness.

—Jennifer Hess, 26, Capital Campaign Coordinator, Portland, Oregon

And Death Shall Have No Dominion

And death shall have no dominion.
Dead men naked they shall be one
With the man in the wind and the west moon;
When their bones are picked clean and the clean bones gone,
They shall have stars at elbow and foot;
Though they go mad they shall be sane,
Though they sink through the sea they shall rise again;
Though lovers be lost love shall not;
And death shall have no dominion.

And death shall have no dominion.
Under the windings of the sea
They lying long shall not die windily;
Twisting on racks when sinews give way,
Strapped to a wheel, yet they shall not break;
Faith in their hands shall snap in two,
And the unicorn evils run them through;
Split all ends up they shan't crack;
And death shall have no dominion.

And death shall have no dominion.
No more may gulls cry at their ears
Or waves break loud on the seashores;
Where blew a flower may a flower no more
Lift its head to the blows of the rain;
Though they be mad and dead as nails,
Heads of the characters hammer through daisies;
Break in the sun till the sun breaks down,
And death shall have no dominion.

RICHARD WILBUR

UNITED STATES • B. 1921

I have mowed lawns around flower beds, and had seen my farmer father chew and clip many a small animal in spring plowing or hay mowing, so I can feel this poem. The fact that it's slightly repulsive to the squeamish gives me guilty pleasure.

—Barbara Germiat, 62, Retired, Appleton, Wisconsin

The Death of a Toad

A toad the power mower caught,
Chewed and clipped of a leg, with a hobbling hop has got
   To the garden verge, and sanctuaried him
   Under the cineraria leaves, in the shade
      Of the ashen heartshaped leaves, in a dim,
         Low, and a final glade.

The rare original heartsblood goes,
Spends on the earthen hide, in the folds and wizenings, flows
   In the gutters of the banked and staring eyes. He lies
   As still as if he would return to stone,
      And soundlessly attending, dies
         Toward some deep monotone,

Toward misted and ebullient seas
And cooling shores, toward lost Amphibia's emperies.
   Day dwindles, drowning, and at length is gone
   In the wide and antique eyes, which still appear
      To watch, across the castrate lawn,
         The haggard daylight steer.

WILLIAM CARLOS WILLIAMS

UNITED STATES • 1883–1963

The Last Words of My English Grandmother

(A shortened version of a poem first published in 1920)

There were some dirty plates
and a glass of milk
beside her on a small table
near the rank, disheveled bed—

Wrinkled and nearly blind
she lay and snored
rousing with anger in her tones
to cry for food,

Gimme something to eat—
They're starving me—
I'm all right I won't go
to the hospital. No, no, no

Give me something to eat
Let me take you
to the hospital, I said
and after you are well

you can do as you please.
She smiled, Yes
you do what you please first
then I can do what I please—

Oh, oh, oh! she cried
as the ambulance men lifted
her to the stretcher—
Is this what you call

making me comfortable?
By now her mind was clear—
Oh you think you're smart
you young people,

she said, but I'll tell you
you don't know anything.
Then we started.
On the way

we passed a long row
of elms. She looked at them
awhile out of
the ambulance window and said,

What are all those
fuzzy-looking things out there?
Trees? Well, I'm tired
of them and rolled her head away.

CHAPTER 4

IN DURANCE
SOUNDLY CAGED

ANONYMOUS

ENGLAND • SIXTEENTH- OR SEVENTEENTH-CENTURY

Mad Tom's Song

From the hag and hungry goblin
    That into rags would rend ye
The spirit that stands by the naked man
    In the book of moons defend ye,
That of your five sound senses
    Ye never be forsaken
Nor wander from yourselves with Tom
    Abroad to beg your bacon.
        While I do sing: "Any food, any feeding,
        Feeding, drink, or clothing?
        Come dame, or maid, be not afraid,
        Poor Tom will injure nothing."

Of thirty bare yeares have I
    Twice twenty been enraged,
And of forty been thrice times fifteen
    In durance soundly caged.
On the lordly lofts of bedlam
    With stubble soft and dainty,
Brave bracelets strong, sweet whips ding-dong,
    And wholesome hunger plenty,
        While I do sing etc.

A thought I took for Maudline
    In a cruse of cockle pottage
With a thing thus tall—God bless you all

I befell into this dotage.
I've slept not since the Conquest,
    Ere then I never waked
Till the roguish fay of love where I lay
    Me found and stripped me naked.
        While I do sing etc.

When I short have shorn my sow's face
    And snigged my hairy barrel
At an oaken inn I pound my skin
    In a suit of gay apparel.
The moon's my constant mistress
    And the lovely owl my marrow
The flaming drake and the night-crow make
    Me music to my sorrow.
        While I do sing etc.

The palsy plague my pulses
    If I prig your pigs or pullen,
Your culvers take, or matchless make
    Your chanticleer or solan!
When I want provant, with Humphry
    I sup and when benighted
I repose in Paul's with walking souls
    And never am affrighted.
        While I do sing etc.

I know more than Apollo
    For oft when he lies sleeping
I see the stars at bloody wars
    And the wounded welkin weeping,
The moon embrace her shepherd,
    And the Queen of Love her warrior,
When the first doth horn the star of the morn
    And the next the heavenly farrier.
        While I do sing etc.

The gypsies Snap and Pedro
    Are none of Tom's camradoes.
The punk I scorn, and cut-purse sworn
    And the roaring-boy's bravadoes.
The meek, the white, the gentle
    Me handle, touch and spare not,
But those that cross Tom Rhinoceros
    Do what the panther dare not.
        While I do sing etc.

With an host of furious fancies
    Whereof I am commander
With a burning spear and a horse of air
    To the wilderness I wander.
By a knight of ghosts and shadows
    I summoned am to tourney
Ten leagues beyond the wide world's end
    Methinks it is no journey.
        While I do sing etc.

I'll bark against the dog-star
    I'll crow away the morning
I'll chase the moon till it be noon
    And make her leave her horning,
But I'll find merry mad Maudline
    And seek whate'er betides her,
And I will love beneath or above
    The dirty earth that hides her.
        While I do sing etc.

W. H. AUDEN

ENGLAND • 1907–1973

*This poem is written in the way I tend to express myself; it's angry, frus-
trated, but oddly quiet, as though the speaker is drained of almost all the
feelings that came with these events and all that remains is but a shadow
of sorrow.*

—Sadie M., 17, Student, Genoa, New York

*I love this poem because it has such vivid and crazy imagery. It's also very
humorous. I especially like the parts about time and how it's always at your
back. To me it captures all the aspects of young love with the crazy foolishness
that goes with it. This poem is a great one to read aloud because it's so much
fun and has a great rhythm.*

—Mishima Alam, 19, Student, Terre Haute, Indiana

As I Walked Out One Evening

As I walked out one evening,
    Walking down Bristol Street,
The crowds upon the pavement
    Were fields of harvest wheat.

And down by the brimming river
    I heard a lover sing
Under an arch of the railway:
    "Love has no ending.

"I'll love you, dear, I'll love you
    Till China and Africa meet,
And the river jumps over the mountain
    And the salmon sing in the street,

"I'll love you till the ocean
    Is folded and hung up to dry
And the seven stars go squawking
    Like geese about the sky.

"The years shall run like rabbits,
    For in my arms I hold
The Flower of the Ages,
    And the first love of the world."

But all the clocks in the city
    Began to whirr and chime:
"O let not Time deceive you,
    You cannot conquer Time.

"In the burrows of the Nightmare
    Where Justice naked is,
Time watches from the shadow
    And coughs when you would kiss.

"In headaches and in worry
    Vaguely life leaks away,
And Time will have his fancy
    Tomorrow or today.

"Into many a green valley
    Drifts the appalling snow;
Time breaks the threaded dances
    And the diver's brilliant bow.

"O plunge your hands in water,
    Plunge them in up to the wrist;
Stare, stare in the basin
    And wonder what you've missed.

"The glacier knocks in the cupboard,
    The desert sighs in the bed,
And the crack in the teacup opens
    A lane to the land of the dead.

"Where the beggars raffle the banknotes
 And the Giant is enchanting to Jack,
And the Lily-white Boy is a Roarer,
 And Jill goes down on her back.

"O look, look in the mirror,
 O look in your distress;
Life remains a blessing
 Although you cannot bless.

"O stand, stand at the window
 As the tears scald and start;
You shall love your crooked neighbour
 With your crooked heart."

It was late, late in the evening,
 The lovers they were gone;
The clocks had ceased their chiming,
 And the deep river ran on.

WILLIAM BLAKE

ENGLAND • 1757–1827

Nurse's Song

(from *Songs of Innocence*)

When the voices of children are heard on the green
And laughing is heard on the hill,
My heart is at rest within my breast
And every thing else is still

Then come home my children, the sun is gone down
And the dews of night arise
Come come leave off play, and let us away
Till the morning appears in the skies

No no let us play, for it is yet day
And we cannot go to sleep
Besides in the sky, the little birds fly
And the hills are all cover'd with sheep

Well well go & play till the light fades away
And then go home to bed
The little ones leaped & shouted & laugh'd
And all the hills echoèd

Nurse's Song

(from *Songs of Experience*)

When the voices of children, are heard on the green
And whisp'rings are in the dale:
The days of my youth rise fresh in my mind,
My face turns green and pale.

Then come home my children, the sun is gone down
And the dews of night arise
Your spring & your day, are wasted in play
And your winter and night in disguise.

The Grey Monk

I die I die the Mother said
My Children die for lack of Bread
What more has the merciless Tyrant said
The Monk sat down on the Stony Bed

The blood red ran from the Grey Monk's side
His hands & feet were wounded wide
His Body bent his arms & knees
Like to the roots of ancient trees

His eye was dry no tear could flow
A hollow groan first spoke his woe
He trembled & shudderd upon the Bed
At length with a feeble cry he said

When God commanded this hand to write
In the studious hours of deep midnight
He told me the writing I wrote should prove
The Bane of all that on Earth I lov'd

My Brother starv'd between two Walls
His Children's Cry my Soul appalls

I mock'd at the wrack & griding chain
My bent body mocks their torturing pain

Thy Father drew his sword in the North
With his thousands strong he marched forth
Thy Brother has armd himself in Steel
To avenge the wrongs thy Children feel

But vain the Sword & vain the Bow
They never can work War's overthrow
The Hermit's Prayer & the Widow's tear
Alone can free the World from fear

For a Tear is an Intellectual Thing
And a Sigh is the Sword of an Angel King
And the bitter groan of the Martyr's woe
Is an Arrow from the Almighty's Bow

The hand of Vengeance found the Bed
To which the Purple Tyrant fled
The iron hand crush'd the Tyrant's head
And became a Tyrant in his stead

GWENDOLYN BROOKS

UNITED STATES • 1917–2000

First fight. Then fiddle. Ply the slipping string . . .

First fight. Then fiddle. Ply the slipping string
With feathery sorcery; muzzle the note
With hurting love; the music that they wrote
Bewitch, bewilder. Qualify to sing
Threadwise. Devise no salt, no hempen thing
For the dear instrument to bear. Devote
The bow to silks and honey. Be remote
A while from malice and from murdering.
But first to arms, to armor. Carry hate
In front of you and harmony behind.
Be deaf to music and to beauty blind.
Win war. Rise bloody, maybe not too late
For having first to civilize a space
Wherein to play your violin with grace.

STERLING A. BROWN

UNITED STATES • 1901–1989

Bitter Fruit of the Tree

They said to my grandmother: "Please do not be bitter,"
When they sold her first-born and let the second die,
When they drove her husband till he took to the swamplands,
And brought him home bloody and beaten at last.
They told her, "It is better you should not be bitter,
Some must work and suffer so that we, who must, can live,
Forgiving is noble, you must not be heathen bitter;
These are your orders: you *are* not to be bitter."
And they left her shack for their porticoed house.

They said to my father: "Please do not be bitter,"
When he ploughed and planted a crop not his,
When he weatherstripped a house that he could not enter,
And stored away a harvest he could not enjoy.
They answered his questions: "It does not concern you,
It is not for you to know, it is past your understanding,
All you need know is: you must not be bitter."
And they laughed on their way to reckon the crop,
And my father walked over the wide garnered acres
Where a cutting wind warned him of the cold to come.

They said to my brother: "Please do not be bitter,
Is it not sad to see the old place go to ruin?
The eaves are sprung and the chimney tower is leaning,
The sills, joists, and columns are rotten in the core;
The blinds hang crazy and the shingles blow away,
The fields have gone back to broomsedge and pine,
And the soil washes down the red gulley scars.
With so much to be done, there's no time for being bitter.
Your father made it for us, it is up to you to save it,
What is past is over, and you should not be bitter."
But my brother is bitter, and he does not hear.

C. P. CAVAFY

GREECE • 1863–1933

Waiting for the Barbarians

What are we waiting for, assembled in the forum?

    The barbarians are due here today.

Why isn't anything going on in the senate?
Why are the senators sitting there without legislating?

    Because the barbarians are coming today.
    What's the point of senators making laws now?
    Once the barbarians are here, they'll do the legislating.

Why did our emperor get up so early,
and why is he sitting enthroned at the city's main gate,
in state, wearing the crown?

    Because the barbarians are coming today
    and the emperor's waiting to receive their leader.
    He's even got a scroll to give him,
    loaded with titles, with imposing names.

Why have our two consuls and praetors come out today
wearing their embroidered, their scarlet togas?
Why have they put on bracelets with so many amethysts,
rings sparkling with magnificent emeralds?
Why are they carrying elegant canes
beautifully worked in silver and gold?

Because the barbarians are coming today
and things like that dazzle the barbarians.

Why don't our distinguished orators turn up as usual
to make their speeches, say what they have to say?

    Because the barbarians are coming today
    and they're bored by rhetoric and public speaking.

Why this sudden bewilderment, this confusion?
(How serious people's faces have become.)
Why are the streets and squares emptying so rapidly,
everyone going home lost in thought?

    Because night has fallen and the barbarians haven't come.
    And some of our men just in from the border say
    there are no barbarians any longer.

Now what's going to happen to us without barbarians?
Those people were a kind of solution.

Translated from the Greek by Edmund Keeley and Philip Sherrard

COUNTEE CULLEN

UNITED STATES • 1903–1946

It leaves a mark on the reader's heart.

—Michael Davis, Reseda, California

This particular poem seemed to mark a change in my consciousness. I first read it as a teen and the joy, beauty, then senselessness and resignation captured an end of my innocence. This poem, crafted so simply, let me know also of the hurts of others, and that I was not alone.

—Norma Patrick-Collier, 37, Librarian, Humboldt, Tennessee

Incident

(For Eric Walrond)

Once riding in old Baltimore,
    Heart-filled, head-filled with glee,
I saw a Baltimorean
    Keep looking straight at me.

Now I was eight and very small,
    And he was no whit bigger,
And so I smiled, but he poked out
    His tongue, and called me, "Nigger."

I saw the whole of Baltimore
    From May until December;
Of all the things that happened there
    That's all that I remember.

EMILY DICKINSON

UNITED STATES • 1830–1886

This poem thrills me by its painful recognition of our human need to be in charge of everything—or else. The letting go is our reluctant acknowledgement that death is the one thing in life we can't control.

—Robert Stevens, 71, Retired, Washington, D.C.

I found this poem in my teens, and was thunderstruck by the third stanza. I've never forgotten it, and have repeated it to myself many times. I can't really describe some of the feelings I have about this poem, but I am grateful that it was written.

—Leslie Evans, 44, Student, Santa Clara, California

After great pain, a formal feeling comes— (341)

After great pain, a formal feeling comes—
The Nerves sit ceremonious, like Tombs—
The stiff Heart questions was it He, that bore,
And Yesterday, or Centuries before?

The Feet, mechanical, go round—
Of Ground, or Air, or Ought—
A Wooden way
Regardless grown,
A Quartz contentment, like a stone—

This is the Hour of Lead—
Remembered, if outlived,
As Freezing persons, recollect the Snow—
First—Chill—then Stupor—then the letting go

RITA DOVE

UNITED STATES • B. 1952

Belinda's Petition

(Boston, February, 1782)

To the honorable Senate and House
of Representatives of this Country,
new born: I am Belinda, an African,
since the age of twelve a Slave.
I will not take too much of your Time,
but to plead and place my pitiable Life
unto the Fathers of this Nation.

Lately your Countrymen have severed
the Binds of Tyranny. I would hope
you would consider the Same for me,
pure Air being the sole Advantage
of which I can boast in my present Condition.

As to the Accusation that I am Ignorant:
I received Existence on the Banks
of the Rio de Valta. All my Childhood
I expected nothing, if that be Ignorance.
The only Travelers were the Dead who returned
from the Ridge each Evening. How might
I have known of Men with Faces like the Moon,
who would ride toward me steadily for twelve Years?

ROBERT FROST

UNITED STATES • 1874–1963

The simplicity of the words and the beautiful sadness proclaimed gently, as if one can hear Frost whispering, make this poem a masterpiece due recognition, as well as a personal favorite.

—James Archer, 19, Bridgeport, West Virginia

Nothing Gold Can Stay

Nature's first green is gold,
Her hardest hue to hold.
Her early leaf's a flower;
But only so an hour.
Then leaf subsides to leaf.
So Eden sank to grief,
So dawn goes down to day.
Nothing gold can stay.

LOUISE GLÜCK

UNITED STATES • B. 1943

The Red Poppy

The great thing
is not having
a mind. Feelings:
oh, I have those; they
govern me. I have
a lord in heaven
called the sun, and open
for him, showing him
the fire of my own heart, fire
like his presence.
What could such glory be
if not a heart? Oh my brothers and sisters,
were you like me once, long ago,
before you were human? Did you
permit yourselves
to open once, who would never
open again? Because in truth
I am speaking now
the way you do. I speak
because I am shattered.

ROBERT HAYDEN

UNITED STATES • 1913–1980

The poem not only celebrates Douglass, but also gives the reader a connection with the past, a promise for the future.

—Lynne Thompson, 47, Human Resources Manager, Los Angeles, California

Frederick Douglass

When it is finally ours, this freedom, this liberty, this beautiful
and terrible thing, needful to man as air,
usable as earth; when it belongs at last to all,
when it is truly instinct, brain matter, diastole, systole,
reflex action; when it is finally won; when it is more
than the gaudy mumbo jumbo of politicians:
this man, this Douglass, this former slave, this Negro
beaten to his knees, exiled, visioning a world
where none is lonely, none hunted, alien,
this man, superb in love and logic, this man
shall be remembered. Oh, not with statues' rhetoric,
not with legends and poems and wreaths of bronze alone,
but with the lives grown out of his life, the lives
fleshing his dream of the beautiful, needful thing.

GERARD MANLEY HOPKINS

ENGLAND • 1844–1889

All of Hopkins's work affects me powerfully, and has done so consistently since I first read his poems in parochial school in about the seventh grade. This poem is not just beautiful—it's heart-wrenchingly beautiful. The poem weeps. If you have ever mourned the felling of a tree, you know the pain the poem delivers. If you have ever witnessed the devastation of an entire avenue or field of trees, you know the exquisite horror Hopkins describes in the poem.

—Martha Gehringer, 53, College Teacher/Writer, Lexington, Kentucky

Binsey Poplars

Felled 1879

My aspens dear, whose airy cages quelled,
Quelled or quenched in leaves the leaping sun,
All felled, felled, are all felled;
    Of a fresh and following folded rank
           Not spared, not one
           That dandled a sandalled
      Shadow that swam or sank
On meadow and river and wind-wandering
      weed-winding bank.

    O if we but knew what we do
          When we delve or hew—
    Hack and rack the growing green!
          Since country is so tender
    To touch, her being só slender,
    That, like this sleek and seeing ball
    But a prick will make no eye at all,

Where we, even where we mean
                To mend her we end her,
                When we hew or delve:
After-comers cannot guess the beauty been.
        Ten or twelve, only ten or twelve
                Strokes of havoc únselve
                        The sweet especial scene,
                Rural scene, a rural scene,
                Sweet especial rural scene.

RANDALL JARRELL

UNITED STATES • 1914–1965

The poem is bleak and beautiful. The word "clambered" in the waking world—a child seeking bed, clumsy as a bear—contrasts with the ease of "sailing" in the dream world. At the apex, the dream world abandons ease, but remains precise. The throat is vividly "starveling," rather than merely thin. The snowflakes "huddle" like the dream-explorer and his dogs. Within the order and variety of iambic pentameter lines, the poet moves between dream world and actual world, between past and present. The lines of the fifth stanza, which begins "And it is meaningless," end with almost rhyming words, all of them ending with "d." Later, different senses of the word "alone" conclude two subsequent lines. The elegant music in the poem, and its formal clarity, create an audible tension with the tangled difficulty it describes.

—M.D.

90 North

At home, in my flannel gown, like a bear to its floe,
I clambered to bed; up the globe's impossible sides
I sailed all night—till at last, with my black beard,
My furs and my dogs, I stood at the northern pole.

There in the childish night my companions lay frozen,
The stiff furs knocked at my starveling throat,
And I gave my great sigh: the flakes came huddling,
Were they really my end? In the darkness I turned to my rest.

—Here, the flag snaps in the glare and silence
Of the unbroken ice. I stand here,
The dogs bark, my beard is black, and I stare
At the North Pole . . .
                And now what? Why, go back.

Turn as I please, my step is to the south.
The world—my world spins on this final point

Of cold and wretchedness: all lines, all winds
End in this whirlpool I at last discover.

And it is meaningless. In the child's bed
After the night's voyage, in that warm world
Where people work and suffer for the end
That crowns the pain—in that Cloud-Cuckoo-Land

I reached my North and it had meaning.
Here at the actual pole of my existence,
Where all that I have done is meaningless,
Where I die or live by accident alone—

Where, living or dying, I am still alone;
Here where North, the night, the berg of death
Crowd me out of the ignorant darkness,
I see at last that all the knowledge

I wrung from the darkness—that the darkness flung me—
Is worthless as ignorance: nothing comes from nothing,
The darkness from the darkness. Pain comes from the darkness
And we call it wisdom. It is pain.

STANLEY KUNITZ

UNITED STATES • B. 1905

This poem reminds me that the struggle is even more majestic, more deeply blessed, precisely because it is blind.

—Robert Ostermeyer, 50, Self-Employed, Cambridge, Massachusetts

King of the River

If the water were clear enough,
if the water were still,
but the water is not clear,
the water is not still,
you would see yourself,
slipped out of your skin,
nosing upstream,
slapping, thrashing,
tumbling
over the rocks
till you paint them
with your belly's blood:
Finned Ego,
yard of muscle that coils,
uncoils.

If the knowledge were given you,
but it is not given,
for the membrane is clouded
with self-deceptions
and the iridescent image swims
through a mirror that flows,
you would surprise yourself
in that other flesh
heavy with milt,
bruised, battering towards the dam
that lips the orgiastic pool.

Come. Bathe in these waters.
Increase and die.

If the power were granted you
to break out of your cells,
but the imagination fails
and the doors of the senses close
on the child within,
you would dare to be changed,
as you are changing now,
into the shape you dread
beyond the merely human.
A dry fire eats you.
Fat drips from your bones.
The flutes of your gills discolor.
You have become a ship for parasites.
The great clock of your life
is slowing down,
and the small clocks run wild.
For this you were born.
You have cried to the wind
and heard the wind's reply:
"I did not choose the way,
the way chose me."
You have tasted the fire on your tongue
till it is swollen black
with a prophetic joy:
"Burn with me!
The only music is time,
the only dance is love."

If the heart were pure enough,
but it is not pure,
you would admit
that nothing compels you
any more, nothing
at all abides,
but nostalgia and desire,

the two-way ladder
between heaven and hell.
On the threshold
of the last mystery,
at the brute absolute hour,
you have looked into the eyes
of your creature self,
which are glazed with madness,
and you say
he is not broken but endures,
limber and firm
in the state of his shining,
forever inheriting his salt kingdom,
from which he is banished
forever.

FEDERICO GARCÍA LORCA

SPAIN • 1898–1936

Lorca wrote the poem in 1929 during an extended visit to New York City, where he felt terribly isolated. As a child, he had lived in the lush region of Andalucia, Spain, in a small, amicable community yet untouched by industrialism. The place was rich with oral tradition—ancient ballads and lullabies were sung to him by nurses and servants. In the poem, the poet recalls the dazzling landscape of his youth, "the place where dream was colliding with reality." The sentence, which is translated well here, "I've seen how things / that seek their way find their void instead," is eerily autobiographical. In 1910, Spain was still a monarchy and Lorca, then twelve years old, was sheltered from the political upheaval that would rip through his country in the coming decades. At the outset of the Spanish Civil War, artists and intellectuals were deemed dangerous by the fascist regime. Lorca was among the first killed in 1936, and his poems and plays were banned for decades under Franco's rule.

—M.D.

1910

(Intermezzo)

Those eyes of mine in nineteen-ten
saw no one dead and buried,
no village fair of ash from the one who weeps at dawn,
no trembling heart cornered like a sea horse.

Those eyes of mine in nineteen-ten
saw the white wall where little girls pissed,
the bull's muzzle, the poisonous mushroom,
and an incomprehensible moon illuminating dried lemon rinds
under the hard black bottles in corners.

Those eyes of mine on the pony's neck,
on the pierced breast of Santa Rosa as she sleeps,
on the rooftops of love, with moans and cool hands,
on a garden where cats devour frogs.

Attic where the ancient dust assembles statues and moss.
Boxes that keep the silence of devoured crabs.
In the place where the dream was colliding with its reality.
My little eyes are there.

Don't ask me any questions. I've seen how things
that seek their way find their void instead.
There are spaces that ache in the uninhabited air
and in my eyes, completely dressed creatures—no one naked there!

Translated from the Spanish by Greg Simon and Steven F. White

ROBERT LOWELL

UNITED STATES • 1917–1977

Much of this work's striking imagery is of places and things around the Boston Common, a place that I know well. I have visited the Gaudens relief described in this poem countless times, which makes the work somehow more meaningful to me. More than that, I love the depth of this poem. It is nearly impossible to unlock its meaning completely with a single, shallow reading. Lowell's work requires careful and thoughtful digging, and I love the challenge of discovery.

—Stefanie Johnson, 20, Student, Tacoma Park, Maryland

For the Union Dead

"Relinquunt Omnia Servare Rem Publicam."

The old South Boston Aquarium stands
in a Sahara of snow now. Its broken windows are boarded.
The bronze weathervane cod has lost half its scales.
The airy tanks are dry.

Once my nose crawled like a snail on the glass;
my hand tingled
to burst the bubbles
drifting from the noses of the cowed, compliant fish.

My hand draws back. I often sigh still
for the dark downward and vegetating kingdom
of the fish and reptile. One morning last March,
I pressed against the new barbed and galvanized

fence on the Boston Common. Behind their cage,
yellow dinosaur steamshovels were grunting
as they cropped up tons of mush and grass
to gouge their underworld garage.

Parking spaces luxuriate like civic
sandpiles in the heart of Boston.

A girdle of orange, Puritan-pumpkin colored girders
braces the tingling Statehouse,

shaking over the excavations, as it faces Colonel Shaw
and his bell-cheeked Negro infantry
on St. Gaudens' shaking Civil War relief,
propped by a plank splint against the garage's earthquake.

Two months after marching through Boston,
half the regiment was dead;
at the dedication,
William James could almost hear the bronze Negroes breathe.

Their monument sticks like a fishbone
in the city's throat.
Its Colonel is as lean
as a compass-needle.

He has an angry wrenlike vigilance,
a greyhound's gentle tautness;
he seems to wince at pleasure,
and suffocate for privacy.

He is out of bounds now. He rejoices in man's lovely,
peculiar power to choose life and die—
when he leads his black soldiers to death,
he cannot bend his back.

On a thousand small town New England greens,
the old white churches hold their air
of sparse, sincere rebellion; frayed flags
quilt the graveyards of the Grand Army of the Republic.

The stone statues of the abstract Union Soldier
grow slimmer and younger each year—
wasp-waisted, they doze over muskets
and muse through their sideburns . . .

Shaw's father wanted no monument
except the ditch,

where his son's body was thrown
and lost with his "niggers."

The ditch is nearer.
There are no statues for the last war here;
on Boylston Street, a commercial photograph
shows Hiroshima boiling

over a Mosler Safe, the "Rock of Ages"
that survived the blast. Space is nearer.
When I crouch to my television set,
the drained faces of Negro school-children rise like balloons.

Colonel Shaw
is riding on his bubble,
he waits
for the blessèd break.

The Aquarium is gone. Everywhere,
giant finned cars nose forward like fish;
a savage servility
slides by on grease.

EDNA ST. VINCENT MILLAY

UNITED STATES • 1892–1950

I discovered this poem in its first printing when it appeared in the New York Times Magazine *on December 28, 1941. I copied it in ink and kept it in my collection of Millay's works ever since that date. I have never seen it in print since. Its theme—the question of how to destroy evil without using evil means yourself—has long been a talisman for my life. This poem has deterred me from taking regrettable steps.*

—Roselle Fine, 78, Psychotherapist, Rochester, New York

Not to Be Spattered by His Blood

(St. George Goes Forth to Slay the Dragon—New Year's, 1942)

Not to be spattered by his blood—this, even then,
This, while I kill him, even then, this, when I slice
His body from his head, must be my nice concern.

This, while I kill him, whom I have hated purely and with all my
        heart, for he is evil,
This, while he dies, for he will strive in death, for he was strong
(I say "was strong," for I shall surely kill him; he is numbered
Already with the dead).

Yes, although now with all his shining scales, the one above the other
        fitted in symmetrical
        —Oh, in most beautiful—design, he moves,
And his long body undulant is looped in many loops most powerfully
        flung from side to side over the world—
Yet is he numbered with the dead, for I shall kill him surely.

Not to be spattered by his blood—this, while I kill him,
Must be my mind's precise concern.

Though the dungeons be empty; though women sit on the door steps
        in the sun

And sigh with peace, because they fear him no more—because they
  fear no one;
And old men in their rocking chairs sing;
And strangers meet in every street of the world and greet each other as
  friends;
And people laugh at anything—

Not here my mission ends.
I must think of my return.
I must kill him with gloves on.

For Hatred is my foe, and I hate him and I will kill him—but oh,
I must kill him with gloves on!

Not to be spattered by his blood—for what, should he be slain,
Done to death by my hand, and my hand be stained
By him, and I bring infection to city and town
And every village in our land—for he spreads quickly—
What then, shall we have gained?
Why then, I say, sooner than that, why, let him live, and me
Lie down!
For it is fitter that a beast be monstrous than that I should be.

Not to be spattered by his blood!—For I know well
What I must conquer.
Can I with seething hatred kill him, and return
And be myself, hating no man.
Once he is dead?

Yes. With God's help, I can.

Not to be spattered by his blood—Oh, God,
In the great hour of my supreme engagement,
Wherein, by Thy just will
And with what strength and skill I can to this endeavor call
I slay our common foe
(For Evil didst Thou never love),
Lest in the end he triumph after all
And what I all but died to kill
Loop his length still

---

192 • *Edna St. Vincent Millay*

Over the world; lest I inherit
Most hated Hate, and be his son in spirit;
And Evil in my veins froth, and I be no one
I ever knew—Oh, God, lest this be done,
Bless Thou my glove!—
This one!
And watch that in the moment of my supreme encounter I wear it, I keep
    it on!

Now, my bright lance, precede me, and lead me to his head.

DOROTHY PARKER

UNITED STATES • 1893–1967

It is so satirical and cold, somehow—yet I find it terribly funny.

—Ellen Prusinski, 18, Student, Grinnell, Iowa

Parker used language as a scalpel and taught me plenty—to the quick.

—Susanne Held, 61, County Government Clerk, Fort Wayne, Indiana

Résumé

Razors pain you;
Rivers are damp;
Acids stain you;
And drugs cause cramp.
Guns aren't lawful;
Nooses give;
Gas smells awful;
You might as well live.

ADRIENNE RICH

UNITED STATES • B. 1929

During my first semester at college, having left the interminable cornfields of the Midwest for the Georgian brick and cobbled walks of Cambridge, I found myself brought up very suddenly against the significance of architecture, both as physical monument and as personal construction. I began to notice the way I moved through buildings, moved in them, entered and left them. At the same time, I was trying to navigate the much less obvious constructions of college life, against whose stately calcifications I felt awkward and inelegant. On one of the first cold nights of the year, an older friend sat me down on the steps facing the library and read me this poem. I could see his breath as he read against the high white clouds in the night sky: intimations of coming storms, of natural forces and the power of environment, set against the immediacy of words.

—Maryanthe Malliaris, 19, Student (Mathematics), Cambridge, Massachusetts

Storm Warnings

The glass has been falling all the afternoon,
And knowing better than the instrument
What winds are walking overhead, what zone
Of gray unrest is moving across the land,
I leave the book upon a pillowed chair
And walk from window to closed window, watching
Boughs strain against the sky

And think again, as often when the air
Moves inward toward a silent core of waiting,
How with a single purpose time has traveled
By secret currents of the undiscerned
Into this polar realm. Weather abroad
And weather in the heart alike come on
Regardless of prediction.

Between foreseeing and averting change
Lies all the mastery of elements
Which clocks and weatherglasses cannot alter.
Time in the hand is not control of time,
Nor shattered fragments of an instrument
A proof against the wind; the wind will rise,
We can only close the shutters.

I draw the curtains as the sky goes black
And set a match to candles sheathed in glass
Against the keyhole draught, the insistent whine
Of weather through the unsealed aperture.
This is our sole defense against the season;
These are the things that we have learned to do
Who live in troubled regions.

EDWIN ARLINGTON ROBINSON

UNITED STATES • 1869–1935

My family never had much money. Dad left when I was five and Mom seemed to work all the time. I still don't know how she did it. I envied the rich famous people I saw on TV. They had it all, and I wanted to be like them—that is, until I read "Richard Cory" in the ninth grade. I had never felt the need to read a poem twice (thinking that most of them were dumb), but I must have read that one a dozen times or more trying to figure out why I found it so moving. The sad story of Richard Cory affected me like no other before or since, making me appreciate just what I DO have— friends, family, and personal fulfillment—if not money or fame.

—Tony Briar, 21, Bookstore Clerk, New Castle, Indiana

I heard this poem for the first time about three years ago. A friend read it to me, and it really hit home. When I was little, my father—a supposedly happy man, a man with a good job, a beautiful baby girl, and a good life ahead of him—killed himself. In the poem, all the people had looked up to Richard Cory. They thought he was wonderful because he was a true gentleman, was always kind and human, and, above all, he was rich. The people strove to be like him so they could be as happy as they thought he was. All along he was the one that was worse off. This poem shows that no matter how wonderful someone may look on the outside, everyone has problems and no one is perfect.

—Amanda King, 19, Student, Barnhart, Missouri

Richard Cory

Whenever Richard Cory went down town,
We people on the pavement looked at him:
He was a gentleman from sole to crown,
Clean favored, and imperially slim.

And he was always quietly arrayed,
And he was always human when he talked;
But still he fluttered pulses when he said,
"Good-morning," and he glittered when he walked.

And he was rich—yes, richer than a king—
And admirably schooled in every grace:
In fine, we thought that he was everything
To make us wish that we were in his place.

So on we worked, and waited for the light,
And went without the meat, and cursed the bread;
And Richard Cory, one calm summer night,
Went home and put a bullet through his head.

ANNE SEXTON

UNITED STATES • 1928–1974

Because I am her kind.

—Jenna McKean, Student, 20, Philadelphia, Pennsylvania

Her Kind

I have gone out, a possessed witch,
haunting the black air, braver at night;
dreaming evil, I have done my hitch
over the plain houses, light by light:
lonely thing, twelve-fingered, out of mind.
A woman like that is not a woman, quite.
I have been her kind.

I have found the warm caves in the woods,
filled them with skillets, carvings, shelves,
closets, silks, innumerable goods;
fixed the suppers for the worms and the elves:
whining, rearranging the disaligned.
A woman like that is misunderstood.
I have been her kind.

I have ridden in your cart, driver,
waved my nude arms at villages going by,
learning the last bright routes, survivor
where your flames still bite my thigh
and my ribs crack where your wheels wind.
A woman like that is not ashamed to die.
I have been her kind.

STEVIE SMITH

ENGLAND • 1902–1971

(1) Like This

(Young man in an Asylum)

It must be some disease I have
To feel so lonely like this,
And not for company I see
The others like this, like this,
It only makes more isolate
To see another like this,
Oh nobody like this *likes* this,
Or likes another like this.

(2) Like This

(Young girl in an Asylum)

The greatest love?
The greatest love?
There is no love at all,
What love means is, To speak to me,
Not leave me in the cold.

How very cold it is out here,
How bitterly the wind blows,
O Love, why did you dedicate me
To the snows?

WALLACE STEVENS

UNITED STATES • 1879–1975

I like it because I have no idea what it means.

—Robert Loy, 41, Police Officer, North Charleston, South Carolina

After reading this poem, I began to understand that something can be said without being labored. In the small group of words—"Let be be finale of seem"—there's a page of conversation. For me, reading it was a wake-up call. I think about that moment the same way I do about my first date with my wife, "Oh, so that's where love begins."

—Garrison Somers, 41, Computer Professional, Chapel Hill, North Carolina

The Emperor of Ice-Cream

Call the roller of big cigars,
The muscular one, and bid him whip
In kitchen cups concupiscent curds.
Let the wenches dawdle in such dress
As they are used to wear, and let the boys
Bring flowers in last month's newspapers.
Let be be finale of seem.
The only emperor is the emperor of ice-cream.

Take from the dresser of deal,
Lacking the three glass knobs, that sheet
On which she embroidered fantails once
And spread it so as to cover her face.
If her horny feet protrude, they come
To show how cold she is, and dumb.
Let the lamp affix its beam.
The only emperor is the emperor of ice-cream.

JEAN TOOMER

UNITED STATES • 1894–1967

I grew up in the South, reaped fields, helped grow and pick cotton. In Toomer's poetry, I experience the mystery and beauty of nature in man's ordinary, yet noble, daily toiling to survive.

—Robert Hinson, 52, Teacher, Indian Trail, North Carolina

Reapers

Black reapers with the sound of steel on stones
Are sharpening scythes. I see them place the hones
In their hip-pockets as a thing that's done,
And start their silent swinging, one by one.
Black horses drive a mower through the weeds,
And there, a field rat, startled, squealing bleeds.
His belly close to ground. I see the blade,
Blood-stained, continue cutting weeds and shade.

WILLIAM CARLOS WILLIAMS

UNITED STATES • 1883–1963

This poem has become a metaphor for these years in prison by reminding me of the hope my future holds. The prison is my winter, purging me of past impurities and of my old self.

—John Cooper, State Prisoner, Norfolk, Massachusetts

By the road to the contagious hospital

By the road to the contagious hospital
under the surge of the blue
mottled clouds driven from the
northeast—a cold wind. Beyond, the
waste of broad, muddy fields
brown with dried weeds, standing and fallen

patches of standing water
the scattering of tall trees

All along the road the reddish
purplish, forked, upstanding, twiggy
stuff of bushes and small trees
with dead, brown leaves under them
leafless vines—

Lifeless in appearance, sluggish
dazed spring approaches—

They enter the new world naked,
cold, uncertain of all
save that they enter. All about them
the cold, familiar wind—

Now the grass, tomorrow
the stiff curl of wildcarrot leaf
One by one objects are defined—
It quickens: clarity, outline of leaf

CHAPTER 5

CURLED AROUND THESE IMAGES

ELIZABETH BISHOP

UNITED STATES • 1911–1979

*An example of how a poet can make unlikely or unpromising material into
the stuff of poetry. "Esso" was a common brand of gas and oil, and "so—
so—so" was something said to soothe nervous horses.*

—R.P.

Filling Station

Oh, but it is dirty!
—this little filling station,
oil-soaked, oil-permeated
to a disturbing, over-all
black translucency.
Be careful with that match!

Father wears a dirty,
oil-soaked monkey suit
that cuts him under the arms,
and several quick and saucy
and greasy sons assist him
(it's a family filling station),
all quite thoroughly dirty.

Do they live in the station?
It has a cement porch
behind the pumps, and on it
a set of crushed and grease-
impregnated wickerwork;
on the wicker sofa
a dirty dog, quite comfy.

Some comic books provide
the only note of color—
of certain color. They lie

upon a big dim doily
draping a taboret
(part of the set), beside
a big hirsute begonia.

Why the extraneous plant?
Why the taboret?
Why, oh why, the doily?
(Embroidered in daisy stitch
with marguerites, I think,
and heavy with gray crochet.)

Somebody embroidered the doily.
Somebody waters the plant,
or oils it, maybe. Somebody
arranges the rows of cans
so that they softly say:
ESSO—SO—SO—SO
to high-strung automobiles.
Somebody loves us all.

LOUISE BOGAN

UNITED STATES • 1897–1970

As Ovid tells it, Medusa was a woman of great beauty, who boasted that she was more beautiful even than the goddess Athena. In a jealous rage, Athena turned her into a Gorgon—a creature with snakes for hair and cold, piercing eyes that could turn a mortal to stone. Here, the encounter with Medusa stops time and renders everything—dust, bell, and grass—immobile, as if the speaker's eyes, once transformed, behold forever the final freeze-frame of her last sight.

—M.D.

Medusa

I had come to the house, in a cave of trees,
Facing a sheer sky.
Everything moved,—a bell hung ready to strike,
Sun and reflection wheeled by.

When the bare eyes were before me
And the hissing hair,
Held up at a window, seen through a door.
The stiff bald eyes, the serpents on the forehead
Formed in the air.

This is a dead scene forever now.
Nothing will ever stir.
The end will never brighten it more than this,
Nor the rain blur.

The water will always fall, and will not fall,
And the tipped bell make no sound.
The grass will always be growing for hay
Deep on the ground.

And I shall stand here like a shadow
Under the great balanced day,
My eyes on the yellow dust, that was lifting in the wind,
And does not drift away.

LUCILLE CLIFTON

UNITED STATES • B. 1936

at last we killed the roaches

at last we killed the roaches.
mama and me. she sprayed,
i swept the ceiling and they fell
dying onto our shoulders, in our hair
covering us with red. the tribe was broken,
the cooking pots were ours again
and we were glad, such cleanliness was grace
when i was twelve. only for a few nights,
and then not much, my dreams were blood
my hands were blades and it was murder murder
all over the place.

H.D. (HILDA DOOLITTLE)

UNITED STATES • 1886–1961

This poem reminds me of how beautiful springtime is. Every year I antici-pate the blooming of those gorgeous pear trees.

—Sheris Bazzetta, 17, Student, Peoria, Illinois

Pear Tree

Silver dust,
lifted from the earth,
higher than my arms reach,
you have mounted,
O, silver,
higher than my arms reach,
you front us with great mass;

no flower ever opened
so staunch a white leaf,
no flower ever parted silver
from such rare silver;

O, white pear,
your flower-tufts
thick on the branch
bring summer and ripe fruits
in their purple hearts.

CARLOS DRUMMOND DE ANDRADE

BRAZIL • 1902–1987

For the plodding profundity of the rhythm (in English anyway), the distance of its gaze, Strand's translation beautifully conveys the tension—upsetting to the ox!—between the nervous, flitting, incomprehensible human world and the slower and more secure rhythms of the animal world.

—Thomas Frick, 48, Editor/Writer, Los Angeles, California

An Ox Looks at Man

They are more delicate even than shrubs and they run
and run from one side to the other, always forgetting
something. Surely they lack I don't know what
basic ingredient, though they present themselves
as noble or serious, at times. Oh, terribly serious,
even tragic. Poor things, one would say that they hear
neither the song of air nor the secrets of hay;
likewise they seem not to see what is visible
and common to each of us, in space. And they are sad,
and in the wake of sadness they come to cruelty.
All their expression lives in their eyes—and loses itself
to a simple lowering of lids, to a shadow.
And since there is little of the mountain about them—
nothing in the hair or in the terribly fragile limbs
but coldness and secrecy—it is impossible for them
to settle themselves into forms that are calm, lasting,
and necessary. They have, perhaps, a kind
of melancholy grace (one minute) and with this they allow
themselves to forget the problems and translucent
inner emptiness that make them so poor and so lacking
when it comes to uttering silly and painful sounds: desire, love,
　　jealousy

(what do we know?)—sounds that scatter and fall in the field
like troubled stones and burn the herbs and the water,
and after this it is hard to keep chewing away at our truth.

Translated from the Portuguese by Mark Strand

ALAN DUGAN

UNITED STATES • B. 1923

Plague of Dead Sharks

Who knows whether the sea heals or corrodes?
The wading, wintered pack-beasts of the feet
slough off, in spring, the dead rind of the shoes'
leather detention, the big toes' yellow horn
shines with a natural polish, and the whole
person seems to profit. The opposite appears
when dead sharks wash up along the beach
for no known reason. What is more built
for winning than the swept-back teeth,
water-finished fins, and pure bad eyes
these old, efficient forms of appetite
are dressed in? Yet it looks as if the sea
digested what it wished of them with viral ease
and threw up what was left to stink and dry.
If this shows how the sea approaches life
in its propensity to feed as animal entire,
then sharks are comforts, feet are terrified,
but they vacation in the mystery and why not?
Who knows whether the sea heals or corrodes?:
what the sun burns up of it, the moon puts back.

T. S. ELIOT

UNITED STATES • 1888–1965

The "Preludes" have stayed with me all these years because they remind me of the days when I was a receptionist and I used to come off work at five o'clock and walk to the subway. There are certain moments in the city that these poems remind me of, and that's why I really love them.

—Suzanne Vega, Singer/Songwriter, New York, New York

It conveys a subtle but intense sadness in its connection to nighttime, something I am aware of in myself—and that same subtle view of the world and my place in it.

—Laura Spero, 18, Student, Bethesda, Maryland

I read Eliot in the seventh grade, San Francisco, 1950. These lines were magic to look at.

—Phyllis Baker, 60, Proofreader, Montesano, Washington

Preludes

I

The winter evening settles down
With smell of steaks in passageways.
Six o'clock.
The burnt-out ends of smoky days.
And now a gusty shower wraps
The grimy scraps
Of withered leaves about your feet
And newspapers from vacant lots;
The showers beat
On broken blinds and chimney-pots,
And at the corner of the street

A lonely cab-horse steams and stamps.
And then the lighting of the lamps.

II

The morning comes to consciousness
Of faint stale smells of beer
From the sawdust-trampled street
With all its muddy feet that press
To early coffee-stands.
With the other masquerades
That time resumes,
One thinks of all the hands
That are raising dingy shades
In a thousand furnished rooms.

III

You tossed a blanket from the bed,
You lay upon your back, and waited;
You dozed, and watched the night revealing
The thousand sordid images
Of which your soul was constituted;
They flickered against the ceiling.
And when all the world came back
And the light crept up between the shutters
And you heard the sparrows in the gutters,
You had such a vision of the street
As the street hardly understands;
Sitting along the bed's edge, where
You curled the papers from your hair,
Or clasped the yellow soles of feet
In the palms of both soiled hands.

IV

His soul stretched tight across the skies
That fade behind a city block,
Or trampled by insistent feet
At four and five and six o'clock;

And short square fingers stuffing pipes,
And evening newspapers, and eyes
Assured of certain certainties,
The conscience of a blackened street
Impatient to assume the world.

I am moved by fancies that are curled
Around these images, and cling:
The notion of some infinitely gentle
Infinitely suffering thing.

Wipe your hand across your mouth, and laugh;
The worlds revolve like ancient women
Gathering fuel in vacant lots.

ROBERT FROST

UNITED STATES • 1874–1963

Watch what is! Forty years ago I first imagined Robert Frost observing this humble drama on his Vermont tablecloth. Since then, I have stretched myself out against the "departmental"—and I confess now with only modest success. But because of this poem I have been more alert than I might have been.

—Palmer Temple, 64, Therapist/Family Minister, Atlanta, Georgia

Departmental

An ant on the tablecloth
Ran into a dormant moth
Of many times his size.
He showed not the least surprise.
His business wasn't with such.
He gave it scarcely a touch,
And was off on his duty run.
Yet if he encountered one
Of the hive's enquiry squad
Whose work is to find out God
And the nature of time and space,
He would put him onto the case.
Ants are a curious race;
One crossing with hurried tread
The body of one of their dead
Isn't given a moment's arrest—
Seems not even impressed.
But he no doubt reports to any
With whom he crosses antennae,
And they no doubt report
To the higher-up at court.
Then word goes forth in Formic:
"Death's come to Jerry McCormic,

Our selfless forager Jerry.
Will the special Janizary
Whose office it is to bury
The dead of the commissary
Go bring him home to his people.
Lay him in state on a sepal.
Wrap him for shroud in a petal.
Embalm him with ichor of nettle.
This is the word of your Queen."
And presently on the scene
Appears a solemn mortician;
And taking formal position,
With feelers calmly atwiddle,
Seizes the dead by the middle,
And heaving him high in air,
Carries him out of there.
No one stands round to stare.
It is nobody else's affair.
It couldn't be called ungentle.
But how thoroughly departmental.

ALLEN GINSBERG

UNITED STATES • 1926–1997

Well, you see, the poem is about this tough, little ugly flower—and I can relate to it. I always appreciate really ugly things. There's something really beautiful about something totally unattractive. It's kind of like me because I act real tough, and I walk and talk real cool, and everyone thinks I'm so detached from everything. But deep down inside I'm really sensitive and I have the form of something more delicate in me.

—Yelina Elkind, 17, Video Store Clerk/Student, Brooklyn, New York

In back of the real

railroad yard in San Jose
    I wandered desolate
in front of a tank factory
    and sat on a bench
near the switchman's shack.

A flower lay on the hay on
    the asphalt highway
—the dread hay flower
    I thought—It had a
brittle black stem and
    corolla of yellowish dirty
spikes like Jesus' inchlong
    crown, and a soiled
dry center cotton tuft
    like a used shaving brush
that's been lying under
    the garage for a year.

Yellow, yellow flower, and
      flower of industry,
tough spiky ugly flower,
      flower nonetheless,
with the form of the great yellow
      Rose in your brain!
This is the flower of the World.

THOM GUNN

ENGLAND • B. 1929

*Though the poem is amusing, the thoughts of the dog are never conde-
scended to—the dog does not seem foolish or inferior, nor is she sentimen-
talized as superior. Rather, she is presented by a convincing act of sympathy
so that she seems real.*

—R.P.

Yoko

All today I lie in the bottom of the wardrobe
feeling low but sometimes getting up
to moodily lumber across rooms
and lap from the toilet bowl, it is so sultry
and then I hear the noise of firecrackers again
all New York is jaggedy with firecrackers today
and I go back to the wardrobe gloomy
trying to void my mind of them.
I am confused, I feel loose and unfitted.

At last deep in the stairwell I hear a tread,
it is him, my leader, my love.
I run to the door and listen to his approach.
Now I can smell him, what a good man he is,
I love it when he has the sweat of work on him,
as he enters I yodel with happiness,
I throw my body up against his, I try to lick his lips,
I care about him more than anything.

After we eat we go for a walk to the piers.
I leap into the standing warmth, I plunge into
the combination of old and new smells.
Here on a garbage can at the bottom, so interesting,
what sister or brother I wonder left this message I sniff.
I too piss there, and go on.

Here a hydrant there a pole
here's a smell I left yesterday, well that's disappointing
but I piss there anyway, and go on.

I investigate so much that in the end
it is for form's sake only, only a drop comes out.

I investigate tar and rotten sandwiches, everything, and go on.

And here a dried old turd, so interesting
so old, so dry, yet so subtle and mellow.
I can place it finely, I really appreciate it,
a gold distant smell like packed autumn leaves in winter
reminding me how what is rich and fierce when excreted
becomes weathered and mild
                              but always interesting
and reminding me of what I have to do.

My leader looks on and expresses his approval.

I sniff it well and later I sniff the air well
a wind is meeting us after the close July day
rain is getting near too but first the wind.
Joy, joy,
being outside with you, active, investigating it all,
with bowels emptied, feeling your approval
and then running on, the big fleet Yoko,
my body in its excellent black coat never lets me down,
returning to you (as I always will, you know that)
and now
         filling myself out with myself, no longer confused,
my panting pushing apart my black lips, but unmoving,
I stand with you braced against the wind.

Considering the Snail

The snail pushes through a green
night, for the grass is heavy
with water and meets over
the bright path he makes, where rain
has darkened the earth's dark. He
moves in a wood of desire,

pale antlers barely stirring
as he hunts. I cannot tell
what power is at work, drenched there
with purpose, knowing nothing.
What is a snail's fury? All
I think is that if later

I parted the blades above
the tunnel and saw the thin
trail of broken white across
litter, I would never have
imagined the slow passion
to that deliberate progress.

ISSA

JAPAN • 1763–1827

The man pulling radishes

The man pulling radishes
pointed my way
    with a radish.

JOHN KEATS

ENGLAND • 1795–1821

I have loved this poem since I first read it long ago because it uncovers so richly and feelingly the abundant pleasure of life—even as the year is dying! Now, of course, it seems to me more poignant and beautiful than ever.

—Matthew Proser, 65, Retired Professor, Mansfield, Connecticut

To Autumn

1

Season of mists and mellow fruitfulness,
    Close bosom-friend of the maturing sun;
Conspiring with him how to load and bless
    With fruit the vines that round the thatch-eaves run;
To bend with apples the mossed cottage-trees,
    And fill all fruit with ripeness to the core;
        To swell the gourd, and plump the hazel shells
    With a sweet kernel; to set budding more,
And still more, later flowers for the bees,
Until they think warm days will never cease,
        For Summer has o'er-brimmed their clammy cells.

2

Who hath not seen thee oft amid thy store?
    Sometimes whoever seeks abroad may find
Thee sitting careless on a granary floor,
    Thy hair soft-lifted by the winnowing wind;
Or on a half-reaped furrow sound asleep,
    Drowsed with the fume of poppies, while thy hook
        Spares the next swath and all its twinéd flowers:
And sometimes like a gleaner thou dost keep
    Steady thy laden head across a brook;
    Or by a cider-press, with patient look,
        Thou watchest the last oozings hours by hours.

3

Where are the songs of Spring? Aye, where are they?
Think not of them, thou hast thy music too—
While barréd clouds bloom the soft-dying day,
And touch the stubble-plains with rosy hue;
Then in a wailful choir the small gnats mourn
Among the river sallows, borne aloft
Or sinking as the light wind lives or dies;
And full-grown lambs loud bleat from hilly bourn;
Hedge crickets sing; and now with treble soft
The redbreast whistles from a garden-croft;
And gathering swallows twitter in the skies.

JANE KENYON

UNITED STATES • 1947–1995

When I read this poem my heart feels lighter. I breathe easier. I get a sense of peace.

—Alan Blender, 50, Technical Recruiter, Bensalem, Pennsylvania

Let Evening Come

Let the light of late afternoon
shine through chinks in the barn, moving
up the bales as the sun moves down.

Let the cricket take up chafing
as a woman takes up her needles
and her yarn. Let evening come.

Let dew collect on the hoe abandoned
in long grass. Let the stars appear
and the moon disclose her silver horn.

Let the fox go back to its sandy den.
Let the wind die down. Let the shed
go black inside. Let evening come.

To the bottle in the ditch, to the scoop
in the oats, to air in the lung
let evening come.

Let it come, as it will, and don't
be afraid. God does not leave us
comfortless, so let evening come.

PHILIP LARKIN

ENGLAND • 1922–1985

It is as perfect and fragile as a snowflake.

—John Ebey, 58, Stockbroker, Santa Monica, California

First Sight

Lambs that learn to walk in snow
When their bleating clouds the air
Meet a vast unwelcome, know
Nothing but a sunless glare.
Newly stumbling to and fro
All they find, outside the fold,
Is a wretched width of cold.

As they wait beside the ewe,
Her fleeces wetly caked, there lies
Hidden round them, waiting too,
Earth's immeasurable surprise.
They could not grasp it if they knew,
What so soon will wake and grow
Utterly unlike the snow.

GAIL MAZUR

UNITED STATES • B. 1937

The connection—or the divorce?—between what we feel ("dislocation") and what we do or see ("the zoo") becomes the heart of a comic but serious meditation, and a series of surprises. Even the poem itself is a kind of surprise, after its title. The couple of animals at the end are closely observed, yet autobiographical.

—R.P.

In Houston

I'd dislocated my life, so I went to the zoo.
It was December but it wasn't December. Pansies
just planted were blooming in well-groomed beds.
Lovers embraced under the sky's Sunday blue.
Children rode around and around on pastel trains.
I read the labels stuck on every cage the way
people at museums do, art being less interesting
than information. Each fenced-in plot had a map,
laminated with a stain to tell where in the world
the animals had been taken from. Rhinos waited
for rain in the rhino-colored dirt, too grief-struck
to move their wrinkles, their horns too weak
to ever be hacked off by poachers for aphrodisiacs.
Five white ducks agitated the chalky waters
of a duck pond with invisible orange feet
while a little girl in pink ruffles
tossed pork rinds at their disconsolate backs.

This wasn't my life! I'd meant to look
with the wise tough eye of exile, I wanted
not to anthropomorphize, not to equate, for instance,
the lemur's displacement with my displacement.
The arched aviary flashed with extravagance,
plumage so exuberant, so implausible, it seemed

cartoonish, and the birdsongs unintelligible,
babble, all their various languages unravelling—
no bird can get its song sung right, separated from
models of its own species.

For weeks I hadn't written a sentence,
for two days I hadn't spoken to an animate thing.
I couldn't relate to a giraffe—
I couldn't look one in the face.
I'd have said, if anyone had asked,
I'd been mugged by the Gulf climate.
In a great barren space, I watched a pair
of elephants swaying together, a rhythm
too familiar to be mistaken, too exclusive.
My eyes sweated to see the bull, his masterful trunk
swinging, enter their barn of concrete blocks,
to watch his obedient wife follow. I missed
the bitter tinny Boston smell of first snow,
the huddling in a cold bus tunnel.

At the House of Nocturnal Mammals,
I stepped into a furtive world of bats,
averted my eyes at the gloomy dioramas,
passed glassed-in booths of lurking rodents—
had I known I'd find what I came for at last?
How did we get here, dear sloth, my soul, my sister?
Clinging to a tree-limb with your three-toed feet,
your eyes closed tight, you calm my idleness,
my immigrant isolation. But a tiny tamarin monkey
who shares your ersatz rainforest runs at you,
teasing, until you move one slow, dripping,
hairy arm, then the other, the other, the other,
pulling your tear-soaked body, its too-few
vertebrae, its inferior allotment of muscles
along the dead branch, going almost nowhere
slowly as is humanly possible, nudged
by the bright orange primate taunting, nipping,
itching at you all the time, like ambition.

EUGENIO MONTALE

ITALY • 1896–1981

During the difficult time of Mussolini's Italy, Montale refused to join the Fascist Party. As a consequence he was dismissed from his position as director of the Scientific-Literary Cabinet, work which gave him time to write. The brilliant sunflower poem celebrates his love of truth as symbolized by the plant that enriches as it worships the light. When we hear the impassioned last line, "Bring me the sunflower crazy with the light," we become the sunny day, the artist, the blazing color, a renewed self.

—Kay Wehner, 75, Copyeditor/Retired Teacher, Berkeley, California

Bring Me the Sunflower

Bring me the sunflower for me to transplant
to my own ground burnt by the spray of sea,
and show all day to the imaging blues
of sky that golden-faced anxiety.

Things hid in darkness lean towards the clear,
bodies consume themselves in a flowing
of shades: and they in varied music—showing
the chance of chances is to disappear.

So bring me the plant that takes you right
where the blond hazes shimmering rise
and life fumes to air as spirit does;
bring me the sunflower crazy with the light.

Translated from the Italian by George Kay

MARIANNE MOORE

UNITED STATES • 1887–1972

It's incredibly beautiful. I don't understand it—I don't have to—I'll read it for the rest of my life and find something different each time, like a favorite painting or film.

—Joy Katz, 35, Graphic Designer/Writer, New York, New York

Those Various Scalpels,

those
various sounds consistently indistinct, like intermingled echoes
    struck from thin glasses successively at random—
        the inflection disguised: your hair, the tails of two
fighting-cocks head to head in stone—
        like sculptured scimitars repeating the curve of your ears in
                                reverse order:
      your eyes, flowers of ice and snow

sown by tearing winds on the cordage of disabled ships; your
                            raised hand,
    an ambiguous signature: your cheeks, those rosettes
      of blood on the stone floors of French châteaux,
    with regard to which the guides are so affirmative—
      your other hand,

a bundle of lances all alike, partly hid by emeralds from Persia
    and the fractional magnificence of Florentine
      goldwork—a collection of little objects—
sapphires set with emeralds, and pearls with a moonstone,
                            made fine

    with enamel in gray, yellow, and dragon-fly blue;
      a lemon, a pear

and three bunches of grapes, tied with silver: your dress, a
                                        magnificent square
        cathedral tower of uniform
            and at the same time diverse appearance—a
        species of vertical vineyard rustling in the storm
            of conventional opinion. Are they weapons or scalpels?
                Whetted to brilliance

by the hard majesty of that sophistication which is superior to
                                                opportunity,
        these things are rich instruments with which to experiment.
            But why dissect destiny with instruments
                more highly specialized than components of destiny itself?

MICHAEL PALMER

UNITED STATES • B. 1943

The Village of Reason

This is a glove
or a book from a book club

This is the sun
or a layer of mud

This is Monday,
this an altered word

This is the village of reason
and this an eye torn out

This is the father
or a number on a chart

This is a substitute,
this the thing you are

This is the varnished picture
or else an accepted response

This is the door
and this the word for door

This is a reflex caused by falling
and this a prisoner with an orange

This is a name you know
and this is the poison to make you well

This is the mechanism
and this the shadow of a bridge

This is a curve
and this its thirst

This is Monday,
this her damaged word

This is the trace
and this the term unmarked

This is the sonnet
and this its burning house

You are in this play
You are its landscape

This is an assumption
the length of an arm

This is a poppy,
this an epilogue

RAINER MARIA RILKE

AUSTRIA • 1875–1926

It is about what beauty is: being fully alive and present, living out of one's center. This poem is so beautiful I can barely stand it. It always challenges me to live more fully.

—Joan L. McGuire, 48, Artist/Hotline Crisis Counselor/Psychotherapist, Austin, Texas

Archaic Torso of Apollo

We cannot know his legendary head
with eyes like ripening fruit. And yet his torso
is still suffused with brilliance from inside,
like a lamp, in which his gaze, now turned to low,

gleams in all its power, Otherwise
the curved breast could not dazzle you so, nor could
a smile run through the placid hips and thighs
to that dark center where procreation flared.

Otherwise this stone would seem defaced
beneath the translucent cascade of the shoulders
and would not glisten like a wild beast's fur:

would not, from all the borders of itself,
burst like a star: for here there is no place
that does not see you. You must change your life.

Translated from the German by Stephen Mitchell

PERCY BYSSHE SHELLEY

ENGLAND • 1792–1822

My favorite poem is one I was forced to memorize as a high school student. At the time I hated it, but over the years it has stuck in my head and its message has grown in significance. Now, as a husband and father I often think of the legacy of Ozymandias, survived only by his "frown, and wrinkled lip, and sneer of cold command," and remember that the only things of permanence are the memories we leave in the hearts of those we love.

—Frank Ahern, 52, Public Relations Representative, Gainesville, Florida

I enjoy reading it over and over because a feeling of knowing a secret of olden times washes over me. This poem makes me think, and I grow excited thinking about the tyrant that never lasts.

—Bronwyn J., 12, Student, Falls Church, Virginia

Ozymandias

I met a traveller from an antique land,
Who said—"Two vast and trunkless legs of stone
Stand in the desert. . . . Near them, on the sand,
Half sunk a shattered visage lies, whose frown,
And wrinkled lip, and sneer of cold command,
Tell that its sculptor well those passions read
Which yet survive, stamped on these lifeless things,
The hand that mocked them, and the heart that fed;
And on the pedestal, these words appear:
My name is Ozymandias, King of Kings,
Look on my Works, ye Mighty, and despair!
Nothing beside remains. Round the decay
Of that colossal Wreck, boundless and bare
The lone and level sands stretch far away."

CHARLES SIMIC

YUGOSLAVIA/UNITED STATES • B. 1938

This poem really hit me when I first read it. I pictured someone like my mother in a struggle to do something simple, then stopping for a quick little laugh in the middle of it all. Simic's poem leaves me with a happy, satisfied sort of feeling. I like that.

—Lauren Mehalik, 18, Student, Strasburg, Pennsylvania

Spring

This is what I saw—old snow on the ground,
Three blackbirds preening themselves,
And my neighbor stepping out in her nightdress
To hang her husband's shirts on the line.

The morning wind made them hard to pin.
It swept the dress so high above her knees,
She had to stop what she was doing
And have a good laugh, while covering herself.

TOM SLEIGH

UNITED STATES • B. 1953

Augusto Jandolo: On Excavating an Etruscan Tomb

"When we lit our torches
My eyes went blind in the cave's
Cool dark—
            the damp rock rough against my palms,
I remember how we strained to lift
                      the great stone lid: slowly
It rose, stood on end . . . then fell
Heavily aside, crashing down
                in the smoky,
Turbulent light
So that just for an instant I saw—
It wasn't a skeleton I saw;
             not bones,
But a body, the arms and legs stiffly outstretched—
A young warrior's flesh still dressed
In armor, with his helmet, spear, shield, and greaves
As though he'd just been laid in the grave:

For just that moment
Inside the sarcophagus I saw the dead live—
                     but then, beneath

The sea-change of our torches,
At the first touch of air, the warrior
Who'd lain there, his body inviolable
For centuries, dissolved—

                       dissolved, as we looked on,
Into dust . . .

            his helmet rolling right, his round shield sagging
Into the void beneath his breastplate, the greaves
Collapsing as his thighs gave way . . .

                        But in the aura
Round our torches a golden powder
Rose up in the glow and seemed to hover."

MARK STRAND

UNITED STATES • B. 1934

Five Dogs

1

I, the dog they call Spot, was about to sing. Autumn
Had come, the walks were freckled with leaves, and a tarnished
Moonlit emptiness crept over the valley floor.
I wanted to climb the poets' hill before the winter settled in;
I wanted to praise the soul. My neighbor told me
Not to waste my time. Already the frost had deepened
And the north wind, trailing the whip of its own scream,
Pressed against the house. "A dog's sublimity is never news,"
He said, "what's another poet in the end?"
And I stood in the midnight valley, watching the great starfields
Flash and flower in the wished-for reaches of heaven.
That's when I, the dog they call Spot, began to sing.

2

Now that the great dog I worshipped for years
Has become none other than myself, I can look within
And bark, and I can look at the mountains down the street
And bark at them as well. I am an eye that sees itself
Look back, a nose that tracks the scent of shadows
As they fall, an ear that picks up sounds
Before they're born. I am the last of the platinum
Retrievers, the end of a gorgeous line.
But there's no comfort being who I am.
I roam around and ponder fate's abolishments

Until my eyes are filled with tears and I say to myself, "Oh Rex,
Forget. Forget. The stars are out. The marble moon slides by."

For Neil Welliver

3

Most of my kind believe that Earth
Is the only planet not covered with hair. So be it,
I say, let tragedy strike, let the story of everything
End today, then let it begin again tomorrow. I no longer care.
I no longer wait in front of the blistered, antique mirror,
Hoping a shape or a self will rise, and step
From that misted surface and say: You there,
Come with me into the world of light and be whole,
For the love you thought had been dead a thousand years
Is back in town and asking for you. Oh no.
I say, I'm done with my kind. I live alone
On Walnut Lane, and will until the day I die.

(After a line of John Ashbery's)

4

Before the tremendous dogs are unleashed,
Let's get the little ones inside, let's drag
The big bones onto the lawn and clean The Royal Dog Hotel.
Gypsy, my love, the end of an age has come. Already,
The howls of the great dogs practicing fills the air,
And look at that man on all fours dancing under
The moon's dumbfounded gaze, and look at that woman
Doing the same. The wave of the future has gotten
To them and they have responded with all they have:
A little step forward, a little step back. And they sway,
And their eyes are closed. O heavenly bodies.
O bodies of time. O golden bodies of lasting fire.

5

All winter the weather came up with amazing results:
The streets and walks had turned to glass. The sky
Was a sheet of white. And here was a dog in a phone booth
Calling home. But nothing would ease his tiny heart.
For years the song of his body was all of his calling. Now
It was nothing. Those hymns to desire, songs of bliss
Would never return. The sky's copious indigo,
The yellow dust of sunlight after rain, were gone.
No one was home. The phone kept ringing. The curtains
Of sleep were about to be drawn, and darkness would pass
Into the world. And so, and so . . . goodbye all, goodbye dog.

DYLAN THOMAS

WALES • 1914–1953

It says almost how I feel in the garden, or when wandering in nature. It feels true, and the details sound beautiful. I loved this poem immediately for its sound, at eighteen, even though it took years to grab its meaning.

—Gwen Cerasoli, 50, Reading Specialist, Highland Park, New Jersey

The Force That through the Green Fuse Drives the Flower

The force that through the green fuse drives the flower
Drives my green age; that blasts the roots of trees
Is my destroyer.
And I am dumb to tell the crooked rose
My youth is bent by the same wintry fever.

The force that drives the water through the rocks
Drives my red blood; that dries the mouthing streams
Turns mine to wax.
And I am dumb to mouth unto my veins
How at the mountain spring the same mouth sucks.

The hand that whirls the water in the pool
Stirs the quicksand; that ropes the blowing wind
Hauls my shroud sail.
And I am dumb to tell the hanging man
How of my clay is made the hangman's lime.

The lips of time leech to the fountain head;
Love drips and gathers, but the fallen blood
Shall calm her sores,
And I am dumb to tell a weather's wind
How time has ticked a heaven round the stars.

And I am dumb to tell the lover's tomb
How at my sheet goes the same crooked worm.

JOSHUA WEINER

UNITED STATES • B. 1963

The poet bases this poem on the children's folk lyric "Fiddle-I-Fee"—a barn-
yard song, where each animal is introduced, then makes a different noise,
each new sound contributing to a longer and longer refrain.

—M.D.

The Yonder Tree

Bought myself a ticket, the ticket freed me,
I flew through a storm to the yonder tree.
      I said to myself   *now I can see, now I can see.*

Bought myself a horse, the horse pleased me,
I rode my horse to the yonder tree.
      The horse said   *nay, nay.*
      I said to myself   *now I can see, now I can see.*

Bought myself a cat, the cat pleased me,
I chased that cat to the yonder tree.
      The cat said   *me, me.*
      The horse said   *nay, nay.*
      I said to myself   *now I can see, now I can see.*

Bought myself a dog, the dog pleased me,
I walked my dog to the yonder tree.
      The dog said   *bow down.*
      The cat said   *me, me.*
      The horse said   *nay, nay.*
      I said to myself   *now I can see, now I can see.*

Found myself a woman, the woman pleased me,
I followed my woman to the yonder tree.
      The woman said   *maybe, baby.*
      The dog said   *bow down.*
      The cat said   *me, me.*

The horse said   *nay, nay.*
I said to myself   *now I can see, now I can see.*

Bought myself a knife, the knife pleased me,
I cut two names into the yonder tree.
    The knife said   *hungry, angry.*
    The woman said   *maybe, baby.*
    The dog said   *bow down.*
    The cat said   *me, me.*
    The horse said   *nay, nay.*
    I said to myself   *now I can see, now I can see.*

Bought myself a house, the house pleased me,
I built my house from the yonder tree.
    The house said   *comfort, come back.*
    The knife said   *hungry, angry.*
    The woman said   *maybe, baby.*
    The dog said   *bow down.*
    The cat said   *me, me.*
    The horse said   *nay, nay.*
    I said to myself   *now I can see, now I can see.*

Bought myself a watch, the watch pleased me,
I checked my watch at the yonder tree.
    The watch said   *tick, take.*
    The house said   *comfort, come back.*
    The knife said   *hungry, angry.*
    The woman said   *maybe, baby.*
    The dog said   *bow down.*
    The cat said   *me, me.*
    The horse said   *nay, nay.*
    I said to myself   *now I can see, now I can see.*

Bought myself a stone, the stone pleased me,
I placed my stone beneath the yonder tree.
    The stone said   *good-night, this night, all night.*
    The watch said   *tick, take.*
    The house said   *comfort, come back.*
    The knife said   *hungry, angry.*

The woman said   *maybe, baby.*
The dog said   *bow down.*
The cat said   *me, me.*
The horse said   *nay, nay.*
I said to myself   *what did I see? I thought I could see . . .*

WALT WHITMAN

UNITED STATES • 1819–1892

A bold, physical poem—if you read it aloud, you can feel the rhythm of repetition in your body. The fourth stanza, one long sentence, unfolds with the rhythm and speed of urgency. The final stanza, where the word "ship" appears six times without tiring, is like a hymn or prayer, Whitman's homage to the voyage he describes.

—M.D.

Aboard at a Ship's Helm

Aboard at a ship's helm,
A young steersman steering with care.

Through fog on a sea-coast dolefully ringing,
An ocean-bell—O a warning bell, rock'd by the waves.

O you give good notice indeed, you bell by the sea-reefs ringing,
Ringing, ringing, to warn the ship from its wreck-place.

For as on the alert O steersman, you mind the loud admonition,
The bows turn, the freighted ship tacking speeds away under her gray
    sails,
The beautiful and noble ship with all her precious wealth speeds away
    gayly and safe.

But O the ship, the immortal ship! O ship aboard the ship!
Ship of the body, ship of the soul, voyaging, voyaging, voyaging.

CHAPTER 6

ALIVE WITH MANY SEPARATE MEANINGS

JOHN ASHBERY

UNITED STATES • B. 1927

The Path to the White Moon

There were little farmhouses there they
Looked like farmhouses yes without very much land
And trees, too many trees and a mistake
Built into each thing rather charmingly
But once you have seen a thing you have to move on

You have to lie in the grass
And play with your hair, scratch yourself
And then the space of this behavior, the air,
Has suddenly doubled
And you have grown to fill the extra place
Looking back at the small, fallen shelter that was

If a stream winds through all this
Alongside an abandoned knitting mill it will not
Say where it has been
The time unfolds like music trapped on the page
Unable to tell the story again
Raging

Where the winters grew white we went outside
To look at things again, putting on more clothes
This too an attempt to define
How we were being in all the surroundings
Big ones sleepy ones
Underwear and hats speak to us
As though we were cats

Dependent and independent
There were shouted instructions
Grayed in the morning

Keep track of us
It gets to be so exciting but so big too
And we have ways to define but not the terms
Yet
We know what is coming, that we are moving
Dangerously and gracefully
Toward the resolution of time
Blurred but alive with many separate meanings
Inside this conversation

JOHN BERRYMAN

UNITED STATES • 1914–1972

The Dream Songs are a strange and moving group of poems, with a series of images and types of talk shared by many of them. I like "14" because it begins "Life, friends, is boring" and goes on to contradict itself.

—Pamela Johnston, 48, Portland, Oregon

Dream Song 14

Life, friends, is boring. We must not say so.
After all, the sky flashes, the great sea yearns,
we ourselves flash and yearn,
and moreover my mother told me as a boy
(repeatingly) "Ever to confess you're bored
means you have no

Inner Resources." I conclude now I have no
inner resources, because I am heavy bored.
Peoples bore me,
literature bores me, especially great literature,
Henry bores me, with his plights & gripes
as bad as achilles,

who loves people and valiant art, which bores me.
And the tranquil hills, & gin, look like a drag
and somehow a dog
has taken itself & its tail considerably away
into mountains or sea or sky, leaving
behind: me, wag.

WILLIAM BLAKE

ENGLAND • 1757–1827

To F——

I mock thee not tho I by thee am Mocked
Thou callst me Madman but I call thee Blockhead

*   *   *

He's a Blockhead who wants a proof of what he Can't Percieve
And he's a Fool who tries to make such a Blockhead believe

*There is no poet who has delivered into human nature an evoked sense of
the uncanny like William Blake. "The Smile" says in four stanzas what a
thousand philosophers could not say in a thousand books.*

—Ralph Dumain, 45, Librarian, Washington, D.C.

The Smile

There is a Smile of Love
And there is a Smile of Deceit
And there is a Smile of Smiles
In which these two Smiles meet

And there is a Frown of Hate
And there is a Frown of Disdain
And there is a Frown of Frowns
Which you strive to forget in vain

For it sticks in the Heart's deep Core
And it sticks in the deep Back bone
And no Smile that ever was smil'd
But only one Smile alone

That betwixt the Cradle & Grave
It only once Smil'd can be
But when it once is Smil'd
There's an end to all Misery

To see a World in a Grain of Sand

To see a World in a Grain of Sand
And a Heaven in a Wild Flower,
Hold Infinity in the palm of your hand
And Eternity in an hour.

GWENDOLYN BROOKS

UNITED STATES • 1917–2000

In 1950, the poet became the first African-American woman to be awarded the Pulitzer Prize, for her book-length poem Annie Allen, *which follows the life of a character by that name. This poem comes out of a section titled "Notes from the Childhood and Girlhood." It's written in rhymed pairs of wildly varying lengths. The poem is wild and ranging, a mind considering the advice that begins the poem.*

—M.D.

"Do not be afraid of no"

"Do not be afraid of no,
Who has so far so very far to go":

New caution to occur
To one whose inner scream set her to cede, for softer lapping
   and smooth fur!

Whose esoteric need
Was merely to avoid the nettle, to not-bleed.

Stupid, like a street
That beats into a dead end and dies there, with nothing left
   to reprimand or meet.

And like a candle fixed
Against dismay and countershine of mixed

Wild moon and sun. And like
A flying furniture, or bird with lattice wing; or gaunt thing,
   a-stammer down a nightmare neon peopled with
   condor, hawk and shrike.

To say yes is to die
A lot or a little. The dead wear capably their wry

Enameled emblems. They smell.
But that and that they do not altogether yell is all that we
            know well.

It is brave to be involved,
To be not fearful to be unresolved.

Her new wish was to smile
When answers took no airships, walked a while.

C. P. CAVAFY

GREECE • 1863–1933

This poem has been a guideline for my life, to embrace every step, and every moment.

—Eleni Chakalos, 71, Dance Director (Greek Folk Dance), Monmouth Beach,
  New Jersey

Better than any other poem I know, it captures the sense of life as an ongoing journey.

—David Millstone, 52, Fifth-Grade Teacher, Lebanon, New Hampshire

This poem makes me feel more sure of not only my own future but the future of this world.

—Kimberley Mitchell, 30, School Principal, Athens, Greece

Ithaka

As you set out for Ithaka
hope your road is a long one,
full of adventure, full of discovery.
Laistrygonians, Cyclops,
angry Poseidon—don't be afraid of them:
you'll never find things like that on your way
as long as you keep your thoughts raised high,
as long as a rare excitement
stirs your spirit and your body.
Laistrygonians, Cyclops,
wild Poseidon—you won't encounter them
unless you bring them along inside your soul,
unless your soul sets them up in front of you.

Hope your road is a long one.
May there be many summer mornings when,
with what pleasure, what joy,
you enter harbors you're seeing for the first time;
may you stop at Phoenician trading stations
to buy fine things,
mother of pearl and coral, amber and ebony,
sensual perfume of every kind—
as many sensual perfumes as you can;
and may you visit many Egyptian cities
to learn and go on learning from their scholars.

Keep Ithaka always in your mind.
Arriving there is what you're destined for.
But don't hurry the journey at all.
Better if it lasts for years,
so you're old by the time you reach the island,
wealthy with all you've gained on the way,
not expecting Ithaka to make you rich.
Ithaka gave you the marvelous journey.
Without her you wouldn't have set out.
She has nothing left to give you now.

And if you find her poor, Ithaka won't have fooled you.
Wise as you will have become, so full of experience,
you'll have understood by then what these Ithakas mean.

Translated from the Greek by Edmund Keeley and Philip Sherrard

RITA DOVE

UNITED STATES • B. 1952

Geometry

I prove a theorem and the house expands:
the windows jerk free to hover near the ceiling,
the ceiling floats away with a sigh.

As the walls clear themselves of everything
but transparency, the scent of carnations
leaves with them. I am out in the open

and above the windows have hinged into butterflies,
sunlight glinting where they've intersected.
They are going to some point true and unproven.

ALAN DUGAN

UNITED STATES • B. 1923

One of the first poems by a living author that dazzled me. It was a revelation to me that words like "ba-bas" and "Lacedaemonians" could work together like this.

—R.P.

How We Heard the Name

The river brought down
dead horses, dead men
and military debris,
indicative of war
or official acts upstream,
but it went by, it all
goes by, that is the thing
about the river. Then
a soldier on a log
went by. He seemed drunk
and we asked him Why
had he and this junk
come down to us so
from the past upstream.
"Friends," he said, "the great
Battle of Granicus
has just been won
by all of the Greeks except
the Lacedaemonians and
myself: this is a joke
between me and a man
named Alexander, whom
all of you ba-bas
will hear of as a god."

GEORGE GASCOIGNE

ENGLAND • 1539–1577

The fifth stanza, which is addressed to the poet's penis, was omitted from
The Oxford Book of English Verse *in editions as late as 1939.*

—R.P.

Gascoigne's Lullaby

Sing lullaby, as women do,
Wherewith they bring their babes to rest,
And lullaby can I sing too
As womanly as can the best.
With lullaby they still the child,
And if I be not much beguiled,
Full many wanton babes have I
Which must be stilled with lullaby.

First, lullaby my youthful years,
It is now time to go to bed,
For crooked age and hoary hairs
Have won the haven within my head;
With lullaby, then, youth be still,
With lullaby, content thy will,
Since courage quails and comes behind,
Go sleep, and so beguile thy mind.

Next, lullaby my gazing eyes,
Which wonted were to glance apace.
For every glass may now suffice
To show the furrows in my face;
With lullaby, then, wink awhile,
With lullaby, your looks beguile,
Let no fair face nor beauty bright
Entice you eft with vain delight.

And lullaby, my wanton will,
Let reason's rule now reign thy thought,
Since all too late I find by skill
How dear I have thy fancies bought;
With lullaby, now take thine ease,
With lullaby, thy doubts appease;
For trust to this, if thou be still,
My body shall obey thy will.

Eke, lullaby my loving boy,
My little Robin, take thy rest;
Since age is cold and nothing coy,
Keep close thy coin, for so is best;
With lullaby, be thou content,
With lullaby, thy lusts relent,
Let others pay which have mo pence,
Thou art too poor for such expense.

Thus lullaby, my youth, mine eyes,
My will, my ware, and all that was!
I can no mo delays devise,
But welcome pain, let pleasure pass;
With lullaby, now take your leave,
With lullaby, your dreams deceive,
And when you rise with waking eye,
Remember Gascoigne's lullaby.

JOHANN WOLFGANG VON GOETHE

GERMANY • 1749–1832

Until I read this in my first quarter of college, I never liked or understood poetry, but this seems to apply so universally to everyone's simultaneous isolation from and connection to the world that it's easy to forget that it was written so long ago.

—Megan Real, 19, Student, Columbus, Ohio

from *Faust, Part 2*

> *The Darkness becomes complete.*

LYNCEUS (*the keeper on the palace watchtower, singing*).

> Sight is my birthright;
> assigned to this tower
> to watch is my task,
> and the world is my joy.
> I gaze into the distance
> or look at what's near—
> the moon and the stars,
> the forest with deer.
> In what I behold
> there always is beauty;
> content with it all,
> I'm content with myself.
> Oh fortunate eyes!
> whatever you've seen,
> whatever the outcome,
> you have known beauty!
> > (*Pause.*)

I have not been stationed here
simply for my private pleasure—
what's this threat of monstrous horror
from the dark world down below!
Through the lindens' twofold night

I see flashing sparks explode;
incandescence, fanned by breezes,
swirls in ever greater rage.
Woe! the fire's in the cottage
that so long was damp with moss;
quick assistance is what's needed,
but no rescuers are near.
Will that dear, that kind old couple,
once so careful with their fires,
be the victims of that smoke!
What a terrible disaster!
Blazing flames—and glowing red
the moss-covered timberwork—
let us hope that those good people
have escaped from the inferno!
Tongues of flashing light are climbing
through the leaves and up the branches;
withered boughs that burn and flicker
soon are blazing, then cave in.
Is this what my eyes should see!
Why must I be so far-sighted?
Now the chapel too collapses,
burdened down by falling branches.
Coiling flames with serpent tongues
have the treetops in their grasp.
To their roots the hollow trunks
blaze scarlet in the glow they cast.—

      (*Long pause. Song.*)

What was once a joy to see
now belongs to ages past.

Translated from the German by Stuart Atkins

JORIE GRAHAM

UNITED STATES • B. 1951

Prayer

Over a dock railing, I watch the minnows, thousands, swirl
themselves, each a minuscule muscle, but also, without the
way to *create* current, making of their unison (turning, re-
                                        infolding,
entering and exiting their own unison in unison) making of
     themselves a
visual current, one that cannot freight or sway by
minutest fractions the water's downdrafts and upswirls, the
dockside cycles of finally-arriving boat-wakes, there where
they hit deeper resistance, water that seems to burst into
itself (it has those layers) a real current though mostly
invisible sending into the visible (minnows) arrowing
                    motion that forces change—
this is freedom. This is the force of faith. Nobody gets
what they want. Never again are you the same. The longing
is to be pure. What you get is to be changed. More and more by
each glistening minute, through which infinity threads itself,
also oblivion, of course, the aftershocks of something
at sea. Here, hands full of sand, letting it sift through
in the wind, I look in and say take this, this is
what I have saved, take this, hurry. And if I listen
now? Listen, I was not saying anything. It was only
something I did. I could not choose words. I am free to go.
I cannot of course come back. Not to this. Never.
It is a ghost posed on my lips. Here: never.

FULKE GREVILLE, LORD BROOKE

ENGLAND • 1554–1628

Greville is one of the great makers of images, as this poem demonstrates. But he also could give tremendous force to abstract terms: "Absence my presence is, strangeness my grace." It's almost a shock to realize that the mighty images and language of this poem all serve the conventional terms of a lover's complaint.

—R.P.

When all this All doth pass from age to age

(*Caelica* 69)

When all this All doth pass from age to age,
And revolution in a circle turn,
Then heavenly justice doth appear like rage,
The caves do roar, the very seas do burn,
    Glory grows dark, the sun becomes a night,
    And makes this great world feel a greater might.

When love doth change his seat from heart to heart,
And worth about the wheel of fortune goes,
Grace is diseas'd, desert seems overthwart,
Vows are forlorn, and truth does credit lose,
    Chance then gives law, desire must be wise,
    And look more ways than one, or lose her eyes.

My age of joy is past, of woes begun,
Absence my presence is, strangeness my grace,
With them that walk against me, is my sun:
The wheel is turn'd, I hold the lowest place,
    What can be good to me since my love is,
    To do me harm, content to do amiss?

ATTILA JÓZSEF

AUSTRIA-HUNGARY • 1905–1937

The Seventh

If you set out in this world,
better be born seven times.
Once, in a house on fire,
once, in a freezing flood,
once, in a wild madhouse,
once, in a field of ripe wheat,
once, in an empty cloister,
and once among pigs in a sty.
Six babes crying, not enough:
you yourself must be the seventh.

When you must fight to survive,
let your enemy see seven.
One, away from work on Sunday,
one, starting his work on Monday,
one, who teaches without payment,
one, who learned to swim by drowning,
one, who is the seed of a forest,
and one, whom wild forefathers protect,
but all their tricks are not enough:
you yourself must be the seventh.

If you want to find a woman,
let seven men go for her.
One, who gives his heart for words,
one, who takes care of himself,

one, who claims to be a dreamer,
one, who through her skirt can feel her,
one, who knows the hooks and snaps,
one, who steps upon her scarf:
let them buzz like flies around her.
You yourself must be the seventh.

If you write and can afford it,
let seven men write your poem.
One, who builds a marble village,
one, who was born in his sleep,
one, who charts the sky and knows it,
one, whom words call by his name,
one, who perfected his soul,
one, who dissects living rats.
Two are brave and four are wise;
you yourself must be the seventh.

And if all went as was written,
you will die for seven men.
One, who is rocked and suckled,
one, who grabs a hard young breast,
one, who throws down empty dishes,
one, who helps the poor to win,
one, who works till he goes to pieces,
one, who just stares at the moon.
The world will be your tombstone:
you yourself must be the seventh.

Translated from the Hungarian by John Balki

PHILIP LEVINE

UNITED STATES • B. 1928

On My Own

Yes, I only got here on my own.
Nothing miraculous. An old woman
opened her door expecting the milk,
and there I was, seven years old, with
a bulging suitcase of wet cardboard
and my hair plastered down and stiff
in the cold. She didn't say, "Come in,"
she didn't say anything. Her luck
had always been bad, so she stood
to one side and let me pass, trailing
the unmistakable aroma of badger
which she mistook for my underwear,
and so she looked upward, not
to heaven but to the cracked ceiling
her husband had promised to mend,
and she sighed for the first time
in my life that sigh which would tell
me what was for dinner. I found my room
and spread my things on the sagging bed:
the bright ties and candy-striped shirts,
the knife to cut bread, the stuffed weasel
to guard the window, the silver spoon
to turn my tea, the pack of cigarettes
for the life ahead, and at last
the little collection of worn-out books
from which I would choose my only name—
Morgan the Pirate, Jack Dempsey, the Prince

of Wales. I chose Abraham Plain
and went off to school wearing a cap
that said "Ford" in the right script.
The teachers were soft-spoken women
smelling like washed babies and the students
fierce as lost dogs, but they all hushed
in wonder when I named the 400 angels
of death, the planets sighted and unsighted,
the moment at which creation would turn
to burned feathers and blow every which way
in the winds of shock. I sat down
and the room grew quiet and warm. My eyes
asked me to close them. I did, and so
I discovered the beauty of sleep and that
to get ahead I need only say I was there,
and everything would open as the darkness
in my silent head opened onto seascapes
at the other end of the world, waves
breaking into mountains of froth, the sand
running back to become the salt savor
of the infinite. Mrs. Tarbox woke me
for lunch—a tiny container of milk
and chocolate cookies in the shape of Michigan.
Of course I went home at 3:30, with
the bells ringing behind me and four stars
in my notebook and drinking companions
on each arm. If you had been there
in your yellow harness and bright hat
directing traffic you would never
have noticed me—my clothes shabby
and my eyes bright—, to you I'd have been
just an ordinary kid. Sure, now you
know, now it's obvious, what with the light
of the Lord streaming through the nine
windows of my soul and the music of rain
following in my wake and the ordinary air
on fire every blessed day I waken the world.

DIONISIO MARTÍNEZ

UNITED STATES • B. 1956

The thoughts in this poem seem to echo to me. Something about Martínez's writing grabs me, sucks me in, makes me love and cry and scream and sigh all at the same time. This is my favorite strophe of the seven-part poem "Flood"—its simplicity is beautiful and the thoughts behind the words are intriguing. Who cannot relate to being alone in the back of a bus or perhaps setting a second place at the dinner table, hoping for unexpected company?

—Laurie Price, 18, Student, Marietta, Georgia

Years of Solitude

To the one who sets a second place at the table anyway.

To the one at the back of the empty bus.

To the ones who name each piece of stained glass projected on a white wall.

To anyone convinced that a monologue is a conversation with the past.

To the one who loses with the deck he marked.

To those who are destined to inherit the meek.

To us.

JAMES McMICHAEL

UNITED STATES • B. 1939

Pretty Blue Apron

0

In the separate histories
wanting writes,

zero doesn't count. Nothing had
happened yet. Zero.

Then it had. There was placental
discharge and infusion. These didn't

follow one another as the night the day,
there wasn't time. With nothing

private for it, undeprived,
the fetus took in everything as

one one one one one without one
"and" between,

without once knowing it was only one.
It got born alive and there one was,

1

a positive and whole number. Into
all one's chances, one unfolds

head first. God only knows the
start it gives one. One has toes.

Reaching for their lost water, each
wiggle of them squeezes through a one-way

pin-hole in time. It's too
much for one to tell that there's an

outside. The heart can't
swell any more toward it and

caves back in,
starts over into every ma-thump mortal

quaver it has left. For all one can
do about it, which is zero, one stays

2

proper to two. No two,
no one. There's second-person

fostering out there somewhere or one leaves.
Two could hardly

bear for one to have to go without.
Born to

see and be seen,
one sees two's face. Two

smiles as she nurses.
When the nipple slips away and isn't

there for awhile,
two's face is there. "There is" is

either of two's nipples, two's one face.
Between one's wanting and the two that gives,

there is a place for things to happen.
Is that look happening that one so wants?

To lack it takes up
one time: two looks, and it

arrives just at one's body at time two. All's
well again, until, again, pressed

forward so that now again, almost
before one lacks it, one's moved

out of the good. Where
is she, that good slaking mother? This one is

looking now again, that's better, good,
one's own smile shows in hers sent

back to one, and so on. After
long enough, there aren't

two mothers anymore, there's one whose
badness one says no to as one also says you

papa, you blue apron, you my lamb.

THEODORE ROETHKE

UNITED STATES • 1908–1963

This poem has spoken to me very directly for more than twenty-five years. The power and truth of it return to me over and over again. It is a celebration of the observance of encountering the countless details that are so frequently overlooked. Being awake to the details makes one's life richer, and this poem points directly to the wonders of being awake.

—Rosette Schureman, 46, Artist, Barneveld, New York

A Field of Light

1

Came to lakes; came to dead water,
Ponds with moss and leaves floating,
Planks sunk in the sand.

A log turned at the touch of a foot;
A long weed floated upward;
An eye tilted.

> Small winds made
> A chilly noise;
> The softest cove
> Cried for sound.

> Reached for a grape
> And the leaves changed;
> A stone's shape
> Became a clam.

> A fine rain fell
> On fat leaves;
> I was there alone
> In a watery drowse.

2

Angel within me, I asked,
Did I ever curse the sun?
Speak and abide.

    Under, under the sheaves,
    Under the blackened leaves,
    Behind the green viscid trellis,
    In the deep grass at the edge of field,
    Along the low ground dry only in August,—

Was it dust I was kissing?
A sigh came far.
Alone, I kissed the skin of a stone;
Marrow-soft, danced in the sand.

3

The dirt left my hand, visitor.
I could feel the mare's nose.
A path went walking.
The sun glittered on a small rapids.
Some morning thing came, beating its wings.
The great elm filled with birds.

    Listen, love,
    The fat lark sang in the field;
    I touched the ground, the ground warmed by the killdeer,
    The salt laughed and the stones;
    The ferns had their ways, and the pulsing lizards,
    And the new plants, still awkward in their soil,
    The lovely diminutives.
    I could watch! I could watch!
    I saw the separateness of all things!
    My heart lifted up with the great grasses;
    The weeds believed me, and the nesting birds.
    There were clouds making a rout of shapes crossing a windbreak
      of cedars,

And a bee shaking drops from a rain-soaked honeysuckle.
The worms were delighted as wrens.
And I walked, I walked through the light air;
I moved with the morning.

JALAL AL-DIN RUMI

PERSIA/TURKEY • 1207–1273

I found this poem a couple months ago in the public library. It speaks to me of freedom and the need to slow down, be still and let your ego die to discover your true self.

—Steve Snyder, 44, Janitorial Service Owner, Tucson, Arizona

Quietness

Inside this new love, die.
Your way begins on the other side.
Become the sky.
Take an axe to the prison wall.
Escape.
Walk out like someone suddenly born into color.
Do it now.
You're covered with thick cloud.
Slide out the side. Die,
and be quiet. Quietness is the surest sign
that you've died.
Your old life was a frantic running
from silence.

The speechless full moon
comes out now.

Translated from the Persian by Coleman Barks

LLOYD SCHWARTZ

UNITED STATES • B. 1941

Proverbs from Purgatory

It was déjà vu all over again.

I know this town like the back of my head.

People who live in glass houses are worth two in the bush.

One hand scratches the other.

A friend in need is worth two in the bush.

A bird in the hand makes waste.

Life isn't all it's crapped up to be.

It's like finding a needle in the eye of the beholder.

It's like killing one bird with two stones.

My motto in life has always been: *Get It Over With.*

Two heads are better than none.

A rolling stone deserves another.

All things wait for those who come.

A friend in need deserves another.

I'd trust him as long as I could throw him.

He smokes like a fish.

He's just a chip off the old tooth.

I'll have him eating out of my lap.

A friend in need opens a can of worms.

Too many cooks spoil the child.

An ill wind keeps the doctor away.

The wolf at the door keeps the doctor away.

People who live in glass houses keep the doctor away.

A friend in need shouldn't throw stones.

A friend in need washes the other.

A friend in need keeps the doctor away.

A stitch in time is only skin deep.

A verbal agreement isn't worth the paper it's written on.

A cat may look like a king.

Know which side of the bed your butter is on.

Nothing is cut and dried in stone.

You can eat more flies with honey than with vinegar.

Don't let the cat out of the barn.

Let's burn that bridge when we get to it.

When you come to a fork in the road, take it.

Don't cross your chickens before they hatch.

DO NOT READ THIS SIGN.

Throw discretion to the wolves.

After the twig is bent, the barn door is locked.

After the barn door is locked, you can come in out of the rain.

A friend in need locks the barn door.

There's no fool like a friend in need.

We've passed a lot of water since then.

At least we got home in two pieces.

All's well that ends.

It ain't over till it's over.

There's always one step further down you can go.

It's a milestone hanging around my neck.

Include me out.

It was déjà vu all over again.

ALAN SHAPIRO

UNITED STATES • B. 1952

Old Joke

Radiant child of Leto, farworking Lord Apollo,
with lyre in hand and golden plectrum, you sang to the gods
on Mount Olympus almost as soon as you were born.

You sang, and the Muses sang in answer, and together
your voices so delighted all your deathless elders
that their perfect happiness was made more perfect still.

What was it, though, that overwhelmed them, that suffused,
astonished, even the endless ether? Was it the freshest,
most wonderful stops of breath, the flawless intervals

and scales whose harmonies were mimicking in sound
the beauty of the gods themselves, or what you joined
to that, what you were singing of, our balked desires,

the miseries we suffer at your indifferent hands,
devastation and bereavement, old age and death?
Farworking, radiant child, what do you know about us?

Here is my father, half blind, and palsied, at the toilet,
he's shouting at his penis, Piss, you! Piss! Piss!
but the penis (like the heavenly host to mortal prayers)

is deaf and dumb; here, too, my mother with her bad knee,
on the eve of surgery, hobbling by the bathroom,
pausing, saying, who are you talking to in there?

and he replies, no one you would know, sweetheart.
Supernal one, in your untested mastery,
your easy excellence, with nothing to overcome,

and needing nothing but the most calamitous
and abject stories to prove how powerful you are,
how truly free, watch them as they laugh so briefly,

godlike, better than gods, if only for a moment
in which what goes wrong is converted to a rightness,
if only because now she's hobbling back to bed

where she won't sleep, if only because he pees at last,
missing the bowl, and has to get down on his knees
to wipe it up. You don't know anything about us.

WALLACE STEVENS

UNITED STATES • 1879–1975

The Pleasures of Merely Circulating

The garden flew round with the angel,
The angel flew round with the clouds,
And the clouds flew round and the clouds flew round
And the clouds flew round with the clouds.

Is there any secret in skulls,
The cattle skulls in the woods?
Do the drummers in black hoods
Rumble anything out of their drums?

Mrs. Anderson's Swedish baby
Might well have been German or Spanish,
Yet that things go round and again go round
Has rather a classical sound.

*This poem is the simplest answer one can give when attempting to find the
meaning of life. Short and rich with sound, it breathes life into "being."
Reading it aloud does it the greatest justice.*

—Leon Calleja, 20, Student, Amherst, Massachusetts

Every time I read it I get chills.

—Rob Pike, 43, Computer Science Researcher, Basking Ridge, New Jersey

Of Mere Being

The palm at the end of the mind,
Beyond the last thought, rises
In the bronze decor,

A gold-feathered bird
Sings in the palm, without human meaning,
Without human feeling, a foreign song.

You know then that it is not the reason
That makes us happy or unhappy.
The bird sings. Its feathers shine.

The palm stands on the edge of space.
The wind moves slowly in the branches.
The bird's fire-fangled feathers dangle down.

WISŁAWA SZYMBORSKA

POLAND • B. 1923

As I've grown up, and especially during the past fifteen years while developing computer programs for business people, I've become aware of the need for most of us to justify and rationalize every move and decision with statistics. Superficial numbers and statistics bring comfort to the illusion that we tightly control the chaos and competition of business. The poem strikes a strong chord with me, because Szymborska understands our need for that illusion. She seems to laugh at our need for numbers—but it's not a cruel laugh.

—Maureen Farrell, 41, Systems Analyst, Plainfield, Indiana

It is so elegantly simple that it can fool a person into thinking it is just a wry numerical categorization of humanity. It is far more spiritual than that. It shames and elevates simultaneously.

—Nancy Suha, 42, Teacher, Mukwonago, Wisconsin

A Contribution to Statistics

Out of a hundred people

those who always know better
—fifty-two,

doubting every step
—nearly all the rest,

glad to lend a hand
if it doesn't take too long
—as high as forty-nine,

always good
because they can't be otherwise
—four, well maybe five,

able to admire without envy
—eighteen,

suffering illusions
induced by fleeting youth
—sixty, give or take a few,

not to be taken lightly
—forty and four,

living in constant fear
of someone or something
—seventy-seven,

capable of happiness
—twenty-something tops,

harmless singly,
savage in crowds
—half at least,

cruel
when forced by circumstances
—better not to know
even ballpark figures,

wise after the fact
—just a couple more
than wise before it,

taking only things from life
—thirty
(I wish I were wrong),

hunched in pain,
no flashlight in the dark
—eighty-three
sooner or later,

righteous
—thirty-five, which is a lot,

righteous
and understanding
—three,

worthy of compassion
—ninety-nine,

mortal
—a hundred out of a hundred.
Thus far this figure still remains unchanged.

Translated from the Polish by Stanislaw Barańczak and Clare Cavanagh

RABINDRANATH TAGORE

INDIA • 1861–1941

Since early childhood I have lived in many countries: India, the U.K., different parts of the Middle East, and now the U.S. In all these cultures, there have been times when I have felt a sudden, frightening sense of alienation, and then, there have been times when the essential similarity of people's values have filled me with a warm sense of belonging. In most situations, this poem has given me strength.

—Jayashree Chaterjee, 52, Librarian, Summit, New Jersey

from *Gitanjali*

35

Where the mind is without fear and the head is held high;
    Where knowledge is free;
    Where the world has not been broken up into fragments by
        narrow domestic walls;
    Where words come out from the depth of truth;
    Where tireless striving stretches its arms towards perfection:
    Where the clear stream of reason has not lost its way into the
        dreary desert sand of dead habit;
    Where the mind is led forward by thee into ever-widening
        thought and action—
Into that heaven of freedom, my Father, let my country awake.

39

When the heart is hard and parched up, come upon me with a shower
    of mercy.
    When grace is lost from life, come with a burst of song.
    When tumultuous work raises its din on all sides shutting me out
        from beyond, come to me, my lord of silence, with thy peace
        and rest.

When my beggarly heart sits crouched, shut up in a corner, break
   open the door, my king, and come with the ceremony of a
   king.
When desire blinds the mind with delusion and dust, O thou
   holy one, thou wakeful, come with thy light and thy thunder.

Translated from the Bengali by Rabindranath Tagore

C. D. WRIGHT

UNITED STATES • B. 1949

Personals

Some nights I sleep with my dress on. My teeth
are small and even. I don't get headaches.
Since 1971 or before, I have hunted a bench
where I could eat my pimento cheese in peace.
If this were Tennessee and across that river, Arkansas,
I'd meet you in West Memphis tonight. We could
have a big time. Danger, shoulder soft.
Do not lie or lean on me. I am still trying to find a job
for which a simple machine isn't better suited.
I've seen people die of money. Look at Admiral Benbow. I wish
like certain fishes, we came equipped with light organs.
Which reminds me of a little known fact:
if we were going the speed of light, this dome
would be shrinking while we were gaining weight.
Isn't the road crooked and steep.
In this humidity, I make repairs by night. I'm not one
among millions who saw Monroe's face
in the moon. I go blank looking at that face.
If I could afford it I'd live in hotels. I won awards
in spelling and the Australian crawl. Long long ago.
Grandmother married a man named Ivan. The men called him
Eve. Stranger, to tell the truth, in dog years I am up there.

CHAPTER 7

I MADE MY SONG A COAT

ANNA AKHMATOVA

RUSSIA • 1889–1966

from *Requiem*

No, not under the vault of alien skies,
And not under the shelter of alien wings—
I was with my people then,
There, where my people, unfortunately, were.

INSTEAD OF A PREFACE

In the terrible years of the Yezhov terror, I spent
seventeen months in the prison lines of Leningrad.
Once, someone "recognized" me. Then a woman with
bluish lips standing behind me, who, of course, had
never heard me called by name before, woke up from
the stupor to which everyone had succumbed and
whispered in my ear (everyone spoke in whispers there):
"Can you describe this?"
And I answered: "Yes, I can."
Then something that looked like a smile passed over
what had once been her face.

Translated from the Russian by Judith Hemschemeyer

FRANK BIDART

UNITED STATES • B.1939

Lament for the Makers

Not bird not badger not beaver not bee

Many creatures must
make, but only one must seek

within itself what to make

My father's ring was a *B* with a dart
through it, in diamonds against polished black stone.

I have it. What parents leave you
is their lives.

Until my mother died she struggled to make
a house that she did not loathe; paintings; poems; me.

Many creatures must

make, but only one must seek
within itself what to make

Not bird not badger not beaver not bee

         *   *   *

Teach me, masters who by making were
remade, your art.

JORGE LUÍS BORGES

ARGENTINA • 1899–1986

Ars Poetica

To look at the river made of time and water
And remember that time is another river,
To know that we are lost like the river
And that faces dissolve like water.

To be aware that waking dreams it is not asleep
While it is another dream, and that the death
That our flesh goes in fear of is that death
Which comes every night and is called sleep.

To see in the day or in the year a symbol
Of the days of man and of his years,
To transmute the outrage of the years
Into a music, a murmur of voices, and a symbol,

To see in death sleep, and in the sunset
A sad gold—such is poetry,
Which is immortal and poor. Poetry
Returns like the dawn and the sunset.

At times in the evenings a face
Looks at us out of the depths of a mirror;
Art should be like that mirror
Which reveals to us our own face.

They say that Ulysses, sated with marvels,
Wept tears of love at the sight of his Ithaca,

Green and humble. Art is that Ithaca
Of green eternity, not of marvels.

It is also like the river with no end
That flows and remains and is the mirror of one same
Inconstant Heraclitus, who is the same
And is another, like the river with no end.

Translated from the Spanish by W. S. Merwin

COUNTEE CULLEN

UNITED STATES • 1903–1946

Would I like poetry so well if it weren't for Countee Cullen? Maybe. But that a middle-aged middle-class stay-at-home mom could be so moved by something written a half-century ago by a young black man—well, that's something. Maybe it's the power of his words in communicating the intoxication of new life. Even in winter, this poem "springs" to mind.

—Amy Whitney, 38, Mother/Part-time Freelance Journalist, Kennesaw, Georgia

To John Keats, Poet, at Spring Time

(For Carl Van Vechten)

I cannot hold my peace, John Keats;
There never was a spring like this;
It is an echo, that repeats
My last year's song and next year's bliss.
I know, in spite of all men say
Of Beauty, you have felt her most.
Yea, even in your grave her way
Is laid. Poor, troubled, lyric ghost,
Spring never was so fair and dear
As Beauty makes her seem this year.

I cannot hold my peace, John Keats,
I am as helpless in the toil
Of Spring as any lamb that bleats
To feel the solid earth recoil
Beneath his puny legs. Spring beats
Her tocsin call to those who love her,
And lo! the dogwood petals cover
Her breast with drifts of snow, and sleek
White gulls fly screaming to her, and hover
About her shoulders, and kiss her cheek,

While white and purple lilacs muster
A strength that bears them to a cluster
Of color and odor; for her sake
All things that slept are now awake.

And you and I, shall we lie still,
John Keats, while Beauty summons us?
Somehow I feel your sensitive will
Is pulsing up some tremulous
Sap road of a maple tree, whose leaves
Grow music as they grow, since your
Wild voice is in them, a harp that grieves
For life that opens death's dark door.
Though dust, your fingers still can push
The Vision Splendid to a birth,
Though now they work as grass in the hush
Of the night on the broad sweet page of the earth.

"John Keats is dead," they say, but I
Who hear your full insistent cry
In bud and blossom, leaf and tree,
Know John Keats still writes poetry.
And while my head is earthward bowed
To read new life sprung from your shroud,
Folks seeing me must think it strange
That merely spring should so derange
My mind. They do not know that you,
John Keats, keep revel with me, too.

EMILY DICKINSON

UNITED STATES • 1830–1886

A poem about writing—or about becoming better-than-amateur at something. It is built out of unexpected contrasts—paste and pearl, gem and sand. "Gem-Tactics" is an example of Dickinson's uncanny gift for invention. It's her made-up term for expertise, for being good at something. She's like a gymnast doing some trick never before seen—flawlessly.

—M.D.

We play at Paste— (320)

We play at Paste—
Till qualified, for Pearl—
Then, drop the Paste—
And deem ourself a fool—

The Shapes—though—were similar—
And our new Hands
Learned *Gem*-Tactics—
Practicing *Sands*—

This poem reminds me of how I feel when I read certain books. I don't even have to leave my room to travel to far-off lands. Reading lets me leave my problems behind.

—Cristina P., 14, Student, Miami, Florida

There is no Frigate like a Book (1263)

There is no Frigate like a Book
To take us Lands away
Nor any Coursers like a Page

Of prancing Poetry—
This Traverse may the poorest take
Without oppress of Toll—
How frugal is the Chariot
That bears the Human soul.

This poem speaks to me of all poetry, and even music lyrics. I agree with
Dickinson, and believe that once they are said, words do not just fade away,
they stay and live on. The poem gives an explanation for why we sometimes
have that little tune or poem playing over and over in our heads.

—Jennifer Day, 18, Student, Miami Shores, Florida

A word is dead (1212)

A word is dead
When it is said,
Some say.

I say it just
Begins to live
That day.

ALLEN GINSBERG

UNITED STATES • 1926–1997

I like this poem's longing for an "America of love." I like the prophetic voices. I like the high tones of the poem that commingle with the lower life of the supermarket.

—Greg Sever, 51, Investor/Househusband, Albuquerque, New Mexico

The poem achieves making the ordinary extraordinary.

—Micah McGuirk, 21, Student, Fort Collins, Colorado

If my favorite means that this is what I remember when I think of poetry, "A Supermarket in California" is mine. It's a combination of all the things that make poetry great—a story, imagination, weirdness, and rhythm.

—Jessica Marler, Memphis, Tennessee

A Supermarket in California

What thoughts I have of you tonight, Walt Whitman, for I walked down the sidestreets under the trees with a headache self-conscious looking at the full moon.

In my hungry fatigue, and shopping for images, I went into the neon fruit supermarket, dreaming of your enumerations!

What peaches and what penumbras! Whole families shopping at night! Aisles full of husbands! Wives in the avocados, babies in the tomatoes!—and you, García Lorca, what were you doing down by the watermelons?

I saw you, Walt Whitman, childless, lonely old grubber, poking among the meats in the refrigerator and eyeing the grocery boys.

I heard you asking questions of each: Who killed the pork chops? What price bananas? Are you my Angel?

I wandered in and out of the brilliant stacks of cans following you, and followed in my imagination by the store detective.

We strode down the open corridors together in our solitary fancy tasting artichokes, possessing every frozen delicacy, and never passing the cashier.

Where are we going, Walt Whitman? The doors close in an hour. Which way does your beard point tonight?

(I touch your book and dream of our odyssey in the supermarket and feel absurd.)

Will we walk all night through solitary streets? The trees add shade to shade, lights out in the houses, we'll both be lonely.

Will we stroll dreaming of the lost America of love past blue automobiles in driveways, home to our silent cottage?

Ah, dear father, graybeard, lonely old courage-teacher, what America did you have when Charon quit poling his ferry and you got out on a smoking bank and stood watching the boat disappear on the black waters of Lethe?

MARK HALLIDAY

UNITED STATES • B. 1949

Get It Again

In 1978 I write something about how
happiness and sorrow are intertwined
and I feel good, insightful, and it seems
this reflects some healthy growth of spirit,
some deep maturation—then
I leaf through an eleven-year-old notebook
and spot some paragraphs I wrote in 1967
on Keats's "Ode on Melancholy" which
seem to say some of it better, or
almost better, or as well though differently—
and the waves roll out, and the waves roll in.

In 1972 I often ate rye toast with peanut butter,
the toast on a blue saucer beside my typewriter,
I took huge bites between paragraphs about love and change;
today it's a green saucer, cream cheese, French bread,
but the motions are the same and in a month or so
when the air is colder I'll be back to my autumn snack,
rye toast with peanut butter, an all-star since '72. . . .
I turned around on sidewalks to stare at women's asses
plenty of times in the sixties and
what do you think will be different in the eighties?
In 1970, mourning an ended love, I listened
to a sailor's song with a timeless refrain,
and felt better—that taste of transcendence
in the night air
and

and here it is in 1978, the night air, hello.

My journalist friend explains the challenge
of his new TV job: you work for a week
to get together one 5-minute feature,
and then
it's gone—
vanished into gray-and-white memory,
a fading choreography of electric dots—
and you're starting it all over,
every week that awesome energy demand:
to start over

In 1973 I played hundreds of games of catch
with a five-year-old boy named Brian.
Brian had trouble counting so we practiced
by counting the times we tossed the ball
without missing. When Brian missed
he was on the verge of despair for a moment
but I taught him to say
"Back to zero!" to give him a sense of
always another chance. I tried to make it sound
exciting to go back to zero, and eventually
our tone was exultant when we shouted in unison
after a bad toss or fumble
back to zero.

In 1977 I wrote a poem called "Repetition Rider"
and last winter I revised it three times
and I thought it was finished.

"It's not like writing," says my journalist friend,
"where your work is permanent—no matter how obscure,
written work is durable. . . . That's why
it can grow—you can move beyond
what you've already said."

Somewhere I read or heard something good
about what Shakespeare meant in *Lear*

when he wrote: "Ripeness is all."
I hope it comes back to me.

I see myself riding
the San Francisco subway in 1974
scrawling something in my little red notebook
about "getting nowhere fast".
I see Brian's big brown eyes lit
with the adventure of starting over
and oblivious, for a moment,
of the extent to which he is
doomed by his disabilities.
And the waves
roll out, and the waves roll in.
This poem

could go on a long time,
but you've already understood it;
you got the point some time ago,

and you'll get it again

LANGSTON HUGHES

UNITED STATES • 1902–1967

Because this poem represents my career as a student, and everything that I value as a human being.

—Drew H., 16, Student

Theme for English B

The instructor said,

> *Go home and write*
> *a page tonight.*
> *And let that page come out of you—*
> *Then, it will be true.*

I wonder if it's that simple?
I am twenty-two, colored, born in Winston-Salem.
I went to school there, then Durham, then here
to this college on the hill above Harlem.
I am the only colored student in my class.
The steps from the hill lead down into Harlem,
through a park, then I cross St. Nicholas,
Eighth Avenue, Seventh, and I come to the Y,
the Harlem Branch Y, where I take the elevator
up to my room, sit down, and write this page:

It's not easy to know what is true for you or me
at twenty-two, my age. But I guess I'm what
I feel and see and hear, Harlem, I hear you:
hear you, hear me—we two—you, me, talk on this page.
(I hear New York, too.) Me—who?
Well, I like to eat, sleep, drink, and be in love.
I like to work, read, learn, and understand life.
I like a pipe for a Christmas present,
or records—Bessie, bop, or Bach.

I guess being colored doesn't make me *not* like
the same things other folks like who are other races.
So will my page be colored that I write?
Being me, it will not be white.
But it will be
a part of you, instructor.
You are white—
yet a part of me, as I am a part of you.
That's American.
Sometimes perhaps you don't want to be a part of me.
Nor do I often want to be a part of you.
But we are, that's true!
I guess you learn from me—
although you're older—and white—
and somewhat more free.

This is my page for English B.

DENISE LEVERTOV

UNITED STATES • 1923–1997

This poem reminds me why we read poetry, go to plays, visit art museums and galleries. It's for that little (or big) "Aha!" when something speaks to us and connects us with the artist and, through him or her, humanity.

—Debbie Thome, Raleigh, North Carolina

The Secret

Two girls discover
the secret of life
in a sudden line of
poetry.

I who don't know the
secret wrote
the line. They
told me

(through a third person)
they had found it
but not what it was
not even

what line it was. No doubt
by now, more than a week
later, they have forgotten
the secret,

the line, the name of
the poem. I love them
for finding what
I can't find,

and for loving me
for the line I wrote,
and for forgetting it
so that

a thousand times, till death
finds them, they may
discover it again, in other
lines

in other
happenings. And for
wanting to know it,
for

assuming there is
such a secret, yes,
for that
most of all.

HEATHER McHUGH

UNITED STATES • B. 1948

A memorable definition of poetry. The emotional power of the poem's conclusion depends upon the nearly talky, nearly gossipy quality of the beginning.

—R.P.

What He Thought

For Fabbio Doplicher

We were supposed to do a job in Italy
and, full of our feeling for
ourselves (our sense of being
Poets from America) we went
from Rome to Fano, met
the mayor, mulled
a couple matters over (what's
cheap date, they asked us; what's
flat drink). Among Italian literati

we could recognize our counterparts:
the academic, the apologist,
the arrogant, the amorous,
the brazen and the glib—and there was one

administrator (the conservative), in suit
of regulation gray, who like a good tour guide
with measured pace and uninflected tone narrated
sights and histories the hired van hauled us past.
Of all, he was most politic and least poetic,
so it seemed. Our last few days in Rome
(when all but three of the New World Bards had flown)
I found a book of poems this
unprepossessing one had written: it was there

---

in the *pensione* room (a room he'd recommended)
where it must have been abandoned by
the German visitor (was there a bus of *them?*)
to whom he had inscribed and dated it a month before.
I couldn't read Italian, either, so I put the book
back into the wardrobe's dark. We last Americans

were due to leave tomorrow. For our parting evening then
our host chose something in a family restaurant, and there
we sat and chatted, sat and chewed,
till, sensible it was our last
big chance to be poetic, make
our mark, one of us asked
                              "What's poetry?
Is it the fruits and vegetables and
marketplace of Campo dei Fiori, or
the statue there?" Because I was

the glib one, I identified the answer
instantly, I didn't have to think—"The truth
is both, it's both," I blurted out. But that
was easy. That was easiest to say. What followed
taught me something about difficulty,
for our underestimated host spoke out,
all of a sudden, with a rising passion, and he said:

The statue represents Giordano Bruno,
brought to be burned in the public square
because of his offense against
authority, which is to say
the Church. His crime was his belief
the universe does not revolve around
the human being: God is no
fixed point or central government, but rather is
poured in waves through all things. All things
move. "If God is not the soul itself, He is
the soul of the soul of the world." Such was
his heresy. The day they brought him

forth to die, they feared he might
incite the crowd (the man was famous
for his eloquence). And so his captors
placed upon his face
an iron mask, in which

he could not speak. That's
how they burned him. That is how
he died: without a word, in front
of everyone.
        And poetry—
                    (we'd all
put down our forks by now, to listen to
the man in gray; he went on
softly)—
        poetry is what

he thought, but did not say.

CZESLAW MILOSZ

POLAND · B. 1911

Incantation

Human reason is beautiful and invincible.
No bars, no barbed wire, no pulping of books,
No sentence of banishment can prevail against it.
It establishes the universal ideas in language,
And guides our hand so we write Truth and Justice
With capital letters, lie and oppression with small.
It puts what should be above things as they are,
Is an enemy of despair and a friend of hope.
It does not know Jew from Greek or slave from master,
Giving us the estate of the world to manage.
It saves austere and transparent phrases
From the filthy discord of tortured words.
It says that everything is new under the sun,
Opens the congealed fist of the past.
Beautiful and very young are Philo-Sophia
And poetry, her ally in the service of the good.
As late as yesterday Nature celebrated their birth,
The news was brought to the mountains by a unicorn and an echo.
Their friendship will be glorious, their time has no limit.
Their enemies have delivered themselves to destruction.

Translated from the Polish by Czeslaw Milosz and Robert Pinsky

FRANK O'HARA

UNITED STATES • 1926–1966

A Step Away from Them

It's my lunch hour, so I go
for a walk among the hum-colored
cabs. First, down the sidewalk
where laborers feed their dirty
glistening torsos sandwiches
and Coca-Cola, with yellow helmets
on. They protect them from falling
bricks, I guess. Then onto the
avenue where skirts are flipping
above heels and blow up over
grates. The sun is hot, but the
cabs stir up the air. I look
at bargains in wristwatches. There
are cats playing in sawdust.
                              On
to Times Square, where the sign
blows smoke over my head, and higher
the waterfall pours lightly. A
Negro stands in a doorway with a
toothpick, languorously agitating.
A blonde chorus girl clicks: he
smiles and rubs his chin. Everything
suddenly honks: it is 12:40 of
a Thursday.
              Neon in daylight is a

great pleasure, as Edwin Denby would
write, as are light bulbs in daylight.
I stop for a cheeseburger at JULIET'S
CORNER. Giulietta Masina, wife of
Federico Fellini, *è bell' attrice.*
And chocolate malted. A lady in
foxes on such a day puts her poodle
in a cab.

      There are several Puerto
Ricans on the avenue today, which
makes it beautiful and warm. First
Bunny died, then John Latouche,
then Jackson Pollock. But is the
earth as full as life was full, of them?
And one has eaten and one walks,
past the magazines with nudes
and the posters for BULLFIGHT and
the Manhattan Storage Warehouse,
which they'll soon tear down. I
used to think they had the Armory
Show there.

      A glass of papaya juice
and back to work. My heart is in my
pocket, it is Poems by Pierre Reverdy.

WALLACE STEVENS

UNITED STATES • 1879–1975

I've read this poem once a week or so for about ten years and find it to be something of a meditation to do so. After all these years I still find myself, after finishing the poem, letting out a little "whew," as the poem has revealed something to me which I had not before seen or realized.

—Wallace Barrett, 46, Chef, Gainesville, Florida

Its stark images always suggest to me that anything and everything can be perceived in yet another way. Turning your head, tuning an attitude, the slightest willingness to see differently, to see with difference, is quietly suggested in the fluid language and imagery.

—Mary Simmons, 43, Teacher/Librarian, Highland, New York

Thirteen Ways of Looking at a Blackbird

I

Among twenty snowy mountains,
The only moving thing
Was the eye of the blackbird.

II

I was of three minds,
Like a tree
In which there are three blackbirds.

III

The blackbird whirled in the autumn winds.
It was a small part of the pantomime.

IV

A man and a woman
Are one.

A man and a woman and a blackbird
Are one.

V

I do not know which to prefer,
The beauty of inflections
Or the beauty of innuendoes,
The blackbird whistling
Or just after.

VI

Icicles filled the long window
With barbaric glass.
The shadow of the blackbird
Crossed it, to and fro.
The mood
Traced in the shadow
An indecipherable cause.

VII

O thin men of Haddam,
Why do you imagine golden birds?
Do you not see how the blackbird
Walks around the feet
Of the women about you?

VIII

I know noble accents
And lucid, inescapable rhythms;
But I know, too,
That the blackbird is involved
In what I know.

IX

When the blackbird flew out of sight,
It marked the edge
Of one of many circles.

X

At the sight of blackbirds
Flying in a green light,
Even the bawds of euphony
Would cry out sharply.

XI

He rode over Connecticut
In a glass coach.
Once, a fear pierced him,
In that he mistook
The shadow of his equipage
For blackbirds.

XII

The river is moving.
The blackbird must be flying.

XIII

It was evening all afternoon.
It was snowing
And it was going to snow.
The blackbird sat
In the cedar-limbs.

MARK STRAND

UNITED STATES • B. 1934

First poem which reaffirmed what nobody was telling me: to read, and that this reading, this consuming is what the imagination feeds on, the soul feeds on.

—Brett Lauer, 20, Student, Brooklyn, New York

Eating Poetry

Ink runs from the corners of my mouth.
There is no happiness like mine.
I have been eating poetry.

The librarian does not believe what she sees.
Her eyes are sad
and she walks with her hands in her dress.

The poems are gone.
The light is dim.
The dogs are on the basement stairs and coming up.

Their eyeballs roll,
their blond legs burn like brush.
The poor librarian begins to stamp her feet and weep.

She does not understand.
When I get on my knees and lick her hand,
she screams.

I am a new man.
I snarl at her and bark.
I romp with joy in the bookish dark.

JAMES TATE

UNITED STATES • B. 1943

I think the point of the poem is that people go about their life, work, social and other everyday activities, and tend to forget about their dreams and aspirations, then wonder what is wrong with their life. They feel like something is missing, like poetry in this poem. It seems to be saying "keep your dreams close to your heart and never let them die."

—Lynn M., 14, Student, Tampa, Florida

Dream On

Some people go their whole lives
without ever writing a single poem.
Extraordinary people who don't hesitate
to cut somebody's heart or skull open.
They go to baseball games with the greatest of ease
and play a few rounds of golf as if it were nothing.
These same people stroll into a church
as if that were a natural part of life.
Investing money is second nature to them.
They contribute to political campaigns
that have absolutely no poetry in them
and promise none for the future.
They sit around the dinner table at night
and pretend as though nothing is missing.
Their children get caught shoplifting at the mall
and no one admits that it is poetry they are missing.
The family dog howls all night,
lonely and starving for more poetry in his life.
Why is it so difficult for them to see
that, without poetry, their lives are effluvial.
Sure, they have their banquets, their celebrations,
croquet, fox hunts, their seashores and sunsets,

their cocktails on the balcony, dog races,
and all that kissing and hugging, and don't
forget the good deeds, the charity work,
nursing the baby squirrels all through the night,
filling the birdfeeders all winter,
helping the stranger change her tire.
Still, there's that disagreeable exhalation
from decaying matter, subtle but ever present.
They walk around erect like champions.
They are smooth-spoken, urbane and witty.
When alone, rare occasion, they stare
into the mirror for hours, bewildered.
There was something they meant to say, but didn't:
"And if we put the statue of the rhinoceros
next to the tweezers, and walk around the room three times,
learn to yodel, shave our heads, call
our ancestors back from the dead—"
poetrywise it's still a bust, bankrupt.
You haven't scribbled a syllable of it.
You're a nowhere man misfiring
the very essence of your life, flustering
nothing from nothing and back again.
The hereafter may not last all that long.
Radiant childhood sweetheart,
secret code of everlasting joy and sorrow,
fanciful pen strokes beneath the eyelids:
all day, all night meditation, knot of hope,
kernel of desire, pure ordinariness of life,
seeking, through poetry, a benediction
or a bed to lie down on, to connect, reveal,
explore, to imbue meaning on the day's extravagant labor.
And yet it's cruel to expect too much.
It's a rare species of bird
that refuses to be categorized.
Its song is barely audible.
It is like a dragonfly in a dream—

here, then there, then here again,
low-flying amber-wing darting upward
and then out of sight.
And the dream has a pain in its heart
the wonders of which are manifold,
or so the story is told.

WILLIAM BUTLER YEATS

IRELAND • 1865–1939

A Coat

I made my song a coat
Covered with embroideries
Out of old mythologies
From heel to throat;
But the fools caught it,
Wore it in the world's eyes
As though they'd wrought it.
Song, let them take it,
For there's more enterprise
In walking naked.

NOTES

CHAPTER 1: THERE WAS A CHILD WENT FORTH

The chapter title is from Walt Whitman's poem of the same title, which appears
on p. 59 of this anthology.

Doty, Mark. "Coastal" is the fifth poem in the six-poem sequence titled "Atlantis"
in the book *Atlantis*.

Winters, Ann. "Night Light" is from a sequence of sonnets titled "Elizabeth Near
and Far" in *Key to the City*.

CHAPTER 2: EITHER WHOM TO LOVE OR HOW

The chapter title is from a section titled "His Excuse for Loving" from Ben Jon-
son's *A Celebration of Charis in Ten Lyric Pieces*, which appears on p. 96 of this
anthology.

Jonson, Ben. "His Excuse for Loving" is the first section of *A Celebration of Charis
in Ten Lyric Pieces*.

Neruda, Pablo, translated by W. S. Merwin. "Tonight I Can Write" is the twenti-
eth poem in *Twenty Love Poems and a Song of Despair*.

Sidney, Sir Philip. "My true love hath my heart and I have his" is a ten-line song that appears in *The Art of English Poesy* (1589). Sidney used the lines as a basis of a sonnet in *The Countess of Pembroke's Arcadia*.

CHAPTER 3: THE FORGETFUL KINGDOM OF DEATH

The chapter title is from "Janet Waking" by John Crowe Ransom, which appears on p. 146 of this anthology.

Chaucer, Geoffrey. "I have of sorwe so grete woon" is from *The Book of the Duchess* (lines 475–485).

Shakespeare, William. "Fear no more the heat o' the sun" is a song from the play *Cymbeline* (Act IV, Scene II).

CHAPTER 4: IN DURANCE SOUNDLY CAGED

The chapter title is from "Mad Tom's Song" (Anonymous), which appears on p. 159 of this anthology.

Brooks, Gwendolyn. "First fight. Then fiddle. Ply the slipping string . . ." is the fourth sonnet in the sequence "The Children of the Poor," from the section titled "The Womanhood" in *Annie Allen*.

Williams, William Carlos. "By the road to the contagious hospital" is the first poem in the sequence "Spring and All."

CHAPTER 5: CURLED AROUND THESE IMAGES

The chapter title is from the fourth section of T. S. Eliot's "Preludes," which appears on p. 216 of this anthology.

CHAPTER 6: ALIVE WITH MANY SEPARATE MEANINGS

The chapter title is from "The Path to the White Moon" by John Ashbery, which appears on p. 253 of this anthology.

Blake, William. The lines appearing here under the title "To see a World in a Grain of Sand" are the first four lines of "Auguries of Innocence," a long verse sequence of aphorisms taken from an 1803 notebook. It's possible that the title referred only to the first four lines.

Martínez, Dionisio. "Years of Solitude" is a selection from the sequence "Flood" in *Bad Alchemy*.

CHAPTER 7: I MADE MY SONG A COAT

The chapter title is from "A Coat" by William Butler Yeats, which appears on p. 327 of this anthology.

PERMISSIONS

Anna Akhmatova, "Instead of a Preface" and epigraph from "Requiem," from *Complete Poems of Anna Akhmatova, Second Edition,* translated by Judith Hemschemeyer. Copyright © 1992 by Judith Hemschemeyer. Reprinted with the permission of Zephyr Press.

Yehuda Amichai, "My Father," translated by Azila Talit Reisenberger, from *Isi-Bongo* 2, No. 1 (January 1997), on-line at http://www.uct.ac.za/projects/poetry/isibongo/vol2-1/hebrew1.htm#Amichai. Reprinted with the permission of the translator.

John Ashbery, "Just Walking Around" and "The Path to the White Moon" from *A Wave* (New York: Viking Press, 1984). Copyright © 1984 by John Ashbery, Reprinted with the permission of Georges Borchardt, Inc., Literary Agency, for the author.

W. H. Auden, "As I Walked Out One Evening" from *W. H. Auden: Collected Poems,* edited by Edward Mendelson. Copyright © 1940 and renewed © 1968 by W. H. Auden. Reprinted with the permission of Random House, Inc.

George Barker, "To My Mother" from *Selected Poems.* Copyright © 1995 by George Barker. Reprinted with the permission of Faber & Faber, Ltd.

Bei Dao, "A Bouquet" from *The August Sleepwalker,* translated by Bonnie S.

Memoir 1969–1980. Copyright © 1987 by Lucille Clifton. Reprinted with the permission of BOA Editions, Ltd.

Frances Cornford, "The Watch" from *Collected Poems* published by Cresset Press. Used by permission of Random House Group Limited.

Countee Cullen, "Incident" and "To John Keats, Poet, at Spring Time" from *On These I Stand: An Anthology of the Best Poems of Countee Cullen*. Copyright © 1925 by Harper & Brothers, renewed © 1953 by Ida M. Cullen. Reprinted with the permission of Thompson and Thompson, for the Estate of Countee Cullen.

E. E. Cummings, "somewhere I have never travelled,gladly beyond" from *Complete Poems 1904–1962*, edited by George J. Firmage. Copyright © 1926, 1954, 1991 by the Trustees for the E. E. Cummings Trust. Copyright © 1985 by George James Firmage. Reprinted with the permission of Liveright Publishing Corporation.

Rubén Darío, "Story for Margarita" ("A Margarita Debayle" from *Intermezzo Tropical y Otras Poemas*) translated by Maggie Dietz. Copyright © 2001. Reprinted with the permission of the translator.

Emily Dickinson, 341 ["After great pain, a formal feeling comes—"], 536 ["The Heart asks Pleasure—first—"], 465 ["I heard a Fly buzz—when I died—"], 320 ["We play at Paste—"], 1212 ["A word is dead"], 1263 ["There is no Frigate like a Book"], 249 ["Wild Nights—Wild Nights!"], and 511 ["If you were coming in the Fall"] from *The Poems of Emily Dickinson*, edited by Thomas H. Johnson. Copyright © 1951, 1955, 1979 by the President and Fellows of Harvard College. Reprinted with the permission of The Belknap Press of Harvard University Press.

H.D. (Hilda Doolittle), "Pear Tree" from *Collected Poems 1912–1944*, edited by Louis L. Martz. Copyright © 1962 by The Estate of Hilda Doolittle. Reprinted with the permission of New Directions Publishing Corporation.

Mark Doty, "Coastal" from *Atlantis*. Copyright © 1995 by Mark Doty. Reprinted with the permission of HarperCollins Publishers, Inc.

Rita Dove, "Belinda's Petition" and "Geometry" from *Selected Poems* (New York: Vintage, 1993). Copyright © 1980 by Rita Dove. Reprinted with the permission of the author.

Carlos Drummond de Andrade, "An Ox Looks at Man," translated by Mark Strand, from *Travelling in the Family*, edited and translated by Thomas Colchie and Mark Strand (New York: The Ecco Press, 1986). Originally in *The New Yorker* (1980). Reprinted with the permission of The Wylie Agency, Inc.

Alan Dugan, "How We Heard the Name" and "Plague of Dead Sharks" from *New*

Stevie Smith. Copyright © 1982 by James MacGibbon. Reprinted with the permission of Farrar, Straus & Giroux, LLC.

Wallace Stevens, "Thirteen Ways of Looking at a Blackbird," "The Emperor of Ice-Cream," "Of Mere Being," and "The Pleasures of Merely Circulating" from *The Collected Poems of Wallace Stevens.* Copyright © 1923 and renewed © 1951 by Wallace Stevens. Reprinted with the permission of Alfred A. Knopf, a division of Random House, Inc.

Mark Strand, "Eating Poetry" from *Selected Poems.* Copyright © 1979, 1980 by Mark Strand. "Five Dogs" from *Blizzard of One.* Copyright © 1998 by Mark Strand. Both reprinted with the permission of Alfred A. Knopf, a division of Random House, Inc.

May Swenson, "Question" from *The Complete Poems to Solve.* Copyright © 1993 by The Literary Estate of May Swenson. Reprinted with the permission of Simon & Schuster Books for Young Readers, an imprint of Simon & Schuster Children's Division.

Wisława Szymborska, "A Contribution to Statistics" from *Poems New and Collected 1957–1997.* English translation by Stanisław Barańczak and Clare Cavanagh. Copyright © 1998 by Harcourt, Inc. Reprinted with the permission of the publishers.

James Tate, "Dream On" from *Shroud of the Gnome* (New York: The Ecco Press, 1997). Copyright © 1997 by James Tate. Reprinted with the permission of HarperCollins Publishers, Inc.

Dylan Thomas, "And death shall have no dominion" and "The Force That Through the Green Fuse Drives the Flower" from *The Poems of Dylan Thomas.* Copyright © 1952 by Dylan Thomas. Reprinted with the permission of New Directions Publishing Corporation and David Higham Associates.

Jean Toomer, "Reapers" from *Cane.* Copyright © 1923 by Boni & Liveright, renewed 1951 by Jean Toomer. Reprinted with the permission of Liveright Publishing Corporation.

Derek Walcott, "Love after Love" from *Collected Poems: 1948–1984.* Copyright © 1984 by Derek Walcott. Reprinted with the permission of Farrar, Straus & Giroux, LLC.

Joshua Weiner, "The Yonder Tree" from *The World's Room* (Chicago: The University of Chicago Press, 2001). Copyright © 2001 by Joshua Weiner. Reprinted with the permission of the author.

E. B. White, "Natural History" from *Poems and Sketches.* Copyright © 1929 by E. B. White. Reprinted with the permission of HarperCollins Publishers, Inc.

Richard Wilbur, "The Death of a Toad" from *Ceremony and Other Poems.* Copy-

INDEX